Praise for
*PAVEd for Success*

"A valuable resource....Teachers will find the lessons in this book engaging and easy to integrate into daily routines."

—**Angela Notari Syverson, Ph.D.**
University of Washington, author of *Ladders to Literacy: A Preschool Activity Book*, *Second Edition*

"An important contribution to early childhood...links research-based principles to concrete practices that early childhood educators can readily use in their classrooms."

—**Shayne B. Piasta, Ph.D.**
The Ohio State University

"Offers clear, concrete examples organized into age-appropriate units of instruction so that teachers will be able to see themselves engaging in the most effective practices to promote and sustain improvements in their students' vocabularies."

—**Rollanda E. O'Connor, Ph.D.**
Professor, University of California, Riverside,
author of *Ladders to Literacy: A Kindergarten Activity Book*, *Second Edition*

"Masterfully translates the research into research-proven lessons that can be implemented successfully in preschool classrooms. A practical resource for teachers."

—**Timothy Shanahan, Ph.D.**
Professor of Urban Education and Director of the Center for Literacy
University of Illinois at Chicago

"An effective and easy-to-follow approach....If you are looking for new ways to expand your early literacy instruction, this is the book for you!"

—**Melanie Kuhn, Ph.D.**
Boston University

"The specific, easy-to-follow, and adaptable lessons described in this gem of a book have been proven to help teachers make great strides in their quest to close the achievement gap."

—**Joseph A. Dimino, Ph.D.**
Senior Research Associate, Instructional Research Group, Los Alamitos, California

"I like *PAVEd for Success* because it was designed in collaboration with preschool and kindergarten teachers in real classroom settings."

—**Sharolyn D. Pollard-Durodola, Ed.D.**
Texas A&M University

"A must read for every preschool and kindergarten teacher...based on exemplary evidence-based research. The book can be used as a curriculum guide and definitely will enhance the vocabulary and language of young children."

—**Lesley M. Morrow, Ph.D.**
Distinguished Professor of Literacy, Rutgers, The State University of New Jersey

"With this program, *all* preschool providers can give young children the foundational knowledge that they need to be successful learners...activities are child-friendly and downright fun!"

—**Elfrieda (Freddy) H. Hiebert**
President/CEO, TextProject & Research Association, University of California, Santa Cruz

# PAVEd
## for Success

# PAVEd
## for Success

Building Vocabulary and
Language Development
in Young Learners

by

**Claire E. Hamilton, Ph.D.**
University of Massachusetts Amherst

and

**Paula J. Schwanenflugel, Ph.D.**
University of Georgia
Athens

·P A U L·H·
BROOKES
PUBLISHING Cº ®

Baltimore • London • Sydney

**Paul H. Brookes Publishing Co.**
Post Office Box 10624
Baltimore, Maryland 21285-0624
USA

www.brookespublishing.com

Typeset by Auburn Associates, Inc., Baltimore, Maryland.
Manufactured in the United States of America by
Versa Press, Inc., East Peoria, Illinois.

The project on which this book is based was funded by Grant S349A010167 from the U.S. Department of Education,
Office of Elementary and Secondary Education, Early Childhood Educator Professional Development Program; and
by Grant ED-06C0-0028 from the U.S. Department of Education, Institute of Education Sciences, National Center
for Education Evaluation and Regional Assistance, administered by the Regional Educational Laboratory Southeast,
administered by the SERVE Center at the University of North Carolina at Greensboro. However, the content does not
necessarily reflect the position of the U.S. Department of Education, and no official endorsement should be inferred.

Teaching Strategies GOLD™ is trademark of Teaching Strategies, Inc.

**Library of Congress Cataloging-in-Publication Data**

Hamilton, Claire E.
    PAVEd for success : building vocabulary and language development in young learners / by Claire E. Hamilton and
Paula J. Schwanenflugel.
        p.    cm.
    Includes bibliographical references.
    ISBN-13: 978-1-59857-172-1
    ISBN-10: 1-59857-172-9
    1. Language arts (Early childhood)    2. Vocabulary—Study and teaching (Early childhood)    I. Schwanenflugel,
Paula J.    II. Title.

LB1139.5.L35H353 2011
372.6'049—dc22                                                                                          2011009017

British Library Cataloguing in Publication data are available from the British Library.

2015    2014    2013    2012    2011

10    9    8    7    6    5    4    3    2    1

# Contents

# Contents of
# the CD-ROM

About This CD-ROM

PAVEd Units

# About the Authors

**Claire E. Hamilton, Ph.D.,** Associate Professor, Department of Teacher Education and Curriculum Studies, School of Education, 217 Furcolo Hall, University of Massachusetts Amherst (UMass Amherst), Amherst, Massachusetts 01003

Dr. Hamilton began her career in early childhood education in the 1980s as a child care teacher. Dr. Hamilton also coordinates the division of Children, Families and Schools at UMass Amherst; and she teaches graduate and undergraduate courses in child development, early childhood education, and elementary education. Her research interests include early literacy, early childhood curriculum, the social context of schooling, and technology-based learning and teaching.

**Paula J. Schwanenflugel, Ph.D.,** Professor of Educational Psychology, Linguistics, and Cognitive Science, 110 Carleton Street, University of Georgia, Athens, Georgia 30602

Dr. Schwanenflugel teaches graduate and undergraduate courses for educators on educational psychology, human development, and psycholinguistics. Her research interests include early literacy, reading fluency, and vocabulary development and their instruction. She has authored or coauthored four books and numerous articles and chapters on early literacy and conceptual development in young children, among other topics.

# Preface

Just a few short years ago, programmatic efforts to create and evaluate programs to enhance the early literacy of young children were rare. Even more unfortunate, many early childhood educators did not have the knowledge and skills they needed to be really up to the task of preparing children with developmentally low early literacy knowledge for school. Every year, legions of young children arrived at kindergarten without the oral language skills needed to learn to read or even communicate effectively with their teachers, despite having attended quality early childhood programs.

In recognition of this problem, the U.S. Department of Education created the Early Childhood Professional Development program, which funded the creation, implementation, and evaluation of a prekindergarten (pre-K) program we called *PAVEd for Success*. The acronym PAVE stands for *p*honological *a*wareness and *v*ocabulary *e*nhancement, which were two of the value-added features we contrasted against a basic early literacy program. Certified teachers in state-funded universal pre-K classrooms in public schools that served ethnically diverse children from families with low to moderate incomes implemented the program.

The *PAVEd for Success* program focused heavily on the development of vocabulary and oral language skills of preschoolers. We took a comprehensive approach to vocabulary by emphasizing research-based classroom practices surrounding interactive storybook reading (which we called *CAR Quest*), teacher–child conversation (*Building Bridges*), and explicit vocabulary practices (*New VEhicles*). We felt that building in a comprehensive approach was important because low vocabulary levels in children tend to be persistent and have long-term effects on learning to read, reading comprehension, and general long-term academic success (Storch & Whitehurst, 2002). The evaluation of this pre-K program (Schwanenflugel et al., 2010) found that a comprehensive treatment of vocabulary was more effective than a less focused one. When other early literacy skills such as phonological awareness and alphabet knowledge were also taught, the program was effective in supporting children with low early literacy skills in the early stages of learning to read a year later in kindergarten.

However, many children enter kindergarten with serious vocabulary needs. The *PAVEd for Success* program was later adapted for kindergarten and modified to enhance its effectiveness based on what we learned from pre-K teachers. This program was evaluated by the Southeastern Regional Education Lab (http://www.serve.org/KPAVEd.aspx) and Abt Associates and funded through the U.S. Department of Education (Goodson, Wolf, Bell, Turner, & Finney, 2010). The kindergarten program was implemented in a large number of kindergarten classrooms in the Mississippi Delta region, and we continued to learn from teachers participating in the program. The evaluation of the kindergarten adaptation of the program continued to indicate its effectiveness for building vocabulary as well as academic knowledge in young learners compared with control approaches.

We feel that most currently available kindergarten reading programs do not at present address oral language skills with the comprehensiveness necessary to dramatically accelerate the development of vocabulary in young children. We think that many kindergarten programs are strong in what has been called *code-related skills* (phonological awareness, alphabet knowledge, structure and uses of print), so these have not been included in PAVE. This program was designed to supplement a more code-focused literacy program and target those skills that underlie vocabulary and oral language. It was designed to be developmentally appropriate for both kindergarten and pre-K instruction.

Observations of teachers' implementation of the program in both pre-K and kindergarten allowed us to learn from teachers how best to structure vocabulary instruction in the classroom. These lessons we learned from teachers regarding how to successfully implement the PAVE vocabulary strategies have been folded into the program we present in this volume. Also included are 24 detailed examples of vocabulary units that address broader goals and topics in the pre-K/kindergarten curriculum, particularly science and social studies standards. Tracking tools are provided to ensure that participation goals for all children are met and communication resources are given for involving parents in vocabulary learning. There are teacher and coach/supervisor checklists for determining whether all components have been met. We have provided concrete ideas for scheduling vocabulary within your existing literacy curriculum and for integrating the program to meet science and social studies goals while teaching vocabulary. In sum, we owe a tremendous debt to teachers for their suggestions and support in developing the *PAVEd for Success* program.

We hope that you and your students will join us in our passion for words. We resonate with this quote from Henry Ward Beecher (Beecher & Drysdale, 1887), who stated, "All words are pegs to hang ideas on." Indeed!

## REFERENCES

Beecher, H.W., & Drysdale, W. (1887). *Proverbs from Plymouth Pulpit.* New York: D. Appleton & Co.

Goodson, B., Wolf, A., Bell, S., Turner, H., & Finney, P.B. (2010). *The effectiveness of a program to accelerate vocabulary development in kindergarten (VOCAB).* (NCEE 2010- 4014). Washington, DC: National Center for Education Evaluation and Regional Assistance, Institute of Education Sciences, U.S. Department of Education.

Schwanenflugel, P.J., Hamilton, C.E., Neuharth-Pritchett, S., Restrepo, M.A., Bradley, B.A., & Webb, M.-Y. (2010). PAVEd for Success: An evaluation of a comprehensive literacy program for 4-year-old children. *Journal of Literacy Research, 42(3),* 227–275.

Storch, S.A., & Whitehurst, G.J. (2002). Oral language and code-related precursors to reading: Evidence from a longitudinal structural model. *Developmental Psychology, 38,* 934–947.

# Acknowledgments

We would like to acknowledge the support of the U.S. Department of Education. This support has been instrumental in funding our efforts toward developing, implementing, and evaluating the prekindergarten (pre-K) and kindergarten *PAVEd for Success* projects. It has allowed us to develop and formalize the program to increase its utility for teachers and its effectiveness for promoting the development of young children's vocabulary. The pilot pre-K program designed for 4-year-olds was developed by Stacey Neuharth-Pritchett, Adelaida Restrepo, and ourselves, with the assistance of a team of energetic and smart doctoral students at the University of Georgia, most notably Barbara Bradley, Jamilia Blake, Janeke Counts, Alicia Marker, Hilary Ruston, and Mi-Young Webb. Their work was invaluable in the original design, implementation, and evaluation of the pre-K program.

We would like to thank the staff, especially the children's librarians, of the Lexington, North Carolina, library. The library served as our summer office and the staff was unfailingly helpful and pleasant in facilitating our work.

Finally, we would like to acknowledge the support and encouragement of our valued colleague, Dr. Marilyn Gootman. We are grateful for her insights and detailed feedback that showed us how to better communicate the program.

*To our children:*
*Paul, Steve, and George,*
*who have grown up while this program was under development*


*To the teachers:*
*the prekindergarten and kindergarten teachers*
*who inspired us and helped us make this program better for children*

# An Introduction to *PAVEd for Success*

**Building Vocabulary and Language Development in Young Learners**

# What Is Early Literacy?

This book is a guide for building a strong foundation for reading during the early childhood years. We have collaborated with classroom teachers to design clear, realistic, practical, and successful strategies that work in real classrooms with real teachers and real students. Our basic premise is that 1) children's later reading success depends to a large degree on a strong foundation, which is built during the preschool and kindergarten years; and that 2) early childhood teachers can easily master skills that will help them fortify this foundation and, thus, make huge strides in bridging the achievement gap. The newly revised guidelines for developmentally appropriate practice suggest, "To be an excellent teacher means…being intentional" (Copple & Bredekamp, 2009, p. 33). The PAVE approach (derived from *p*honological *a*wareness and *v*ocabulary *e*nhancement) is designed to help preschool and kindergarten teachers build children's vocabulary and oral language skills with intentionality.

Because thoughtful, thorough research underlies every successful educational practice, in this chapter we explore the research that underlies the development of the *PAVEd for Success* program. First we look at how this program coincides with research on early literacy in general, and then we describe the specific research process behind *PAVEd for Success*.

## LITERACY RESEARCH

The basic language and cognitive early literacy competencies that children need to become good readers are called *foundational skills*; that is, they lay the foundation for formal reading instruction. Research confirms what we know instinctively—a strong foundation of language and cognitive competencies or skills leads to strong literacy skills once formal literacy (reading) instruction begins. A weak foundation crumbles when formal literacy instruction begins, potentially placing children at risk for early reading difficulties (Whitehurst & Lonigan, 1998).

But what does research say about the specific literacy skills teachers should focus on in their prekindergarten (pre-K) and kindergarten classrooms? Early literacy is composed of two interrelated sets of underlying abilities: 1) code-related skills and 2) oral language skills

(National Early Literacy Panel, 2009). Code-related skills allow children to crack the code for deciphering the written word and include skills such as learning the letters of the alphabet and phonics rules. Children who have these skills prior to learning to read do better on early assessments of reading than children starting out with poor knowledge in these areas. All quality early childhood programs should provide children with instruction in these literacy areas. Code-related skills are relatively small sets of knowledge that can be mastered rather quickly by most children in a year or two. After all, there are only 26 letters in the English alphabet, and some people estimate that the number of reliable phonics rules that children need to be taught might be as small as 18 (Clymer, 1963)! In our experience, many early literacy programs do a pretty good job of teaching these skills, so we do not focus on them here. However, we include in Appendix B an annotated list of resources for teachers who would like more information on early literacy in general and code-related skills in particular.

However, research also suggests that attending to code-related skills may not be enough to ensure early reading success. Although teaching code-related skills may help children learn how to read words, it does not fully prepare them to tackle the main goal of reading—comprehending text. That's where oral language skills, the other set of underlying abilities for early literacy, come in. Oral language skills include comprehending and producing complex sentences, inferring (i.e., determining important information not stated directly in the text but necessary for comprehension), general listening abilities, and—perhaps most important—vocabulary skills. Indeed, it appears that oral language skills in and of themselves underpin reading and listening comprehension during kindergarten and preschool (Lynch et al., 2008). In our experience, many early literacy programs do not focus nearly enough on oral language skills.

Although children can master code-related skills in a year or two, oral language skills are continually developed throughout one's lifetime. They are much more complicated because they require both the integration of vocabulary, oral, and written language skills and an underlying and expanding knowledge base. Because of this extended developmental time frame, oral language problems can be more long lasting (Paris, 2005). Children with insufficient oral language may struggle in later grades as they encounter what Stahl called "heavy texts" (2007, p. 56), or long books with well-developed themes, complex plots and sentence structure, and complex vocabulary. Thus, it makes sense that teachers get as early a start as possible on improving their students' vocabulary and oral language skills.

Vocabulary is important even for such a "simple" thing as reading words. "A child just learning to read conventionally might approach [a] word...by sounding it out...Not infrequently, one can hear a beginning reader get that far and be stumped, even though all the letters have been sounded out correctly" (Whitehurst & Lonigan, 1998, p. 849). In reading, young children must be able to map the written letters and sounds of a word onto the meaning of a word they know. When children have difficulty retrieving the meaning of a particular word they have successfully sounded out, comprehension (Stahl, 1999) and word recognition (Nation & Snowling, 2004; Schwanenflugel & Noyes, 1996) suffer. Vocabulary, then, is important for every aspect of learning to read.

As researchers, we are still trying to untangle the relationship between preschool vocabulary and oral language skills and later reading ability. Different researchers have different findings, but all agree that vocabulary is critical. Some researchers have found that although children with good vocabularies tend to be better readers, vocabulary skills do not say much about who will end up a good reader once phonics and alphabet skills are taken into account (Muter, Hulme, Snowling, & Stevenson, 2004). Others have found that both vocabulary knowledge and oral language skills are important in learning to read (Dickinson, McCabe, Anastasopoulos, Peisner-Feinberg, & Poe, 2003). The National Institute of Child Health and Human Development (NICHD) Early Child Care Research Network (2005) followed 1,100 children from age 3 to third grade. This large study found that preschool oral language skills helped children to learn code-related skills as well as build later reading comprehension. Yet other theories say that preschool oral language and vocabulary skills operate by helping children discriminate words by sound (e.g., consider the distinction between the words *bait* and *bat*), which later helps them learn to read (Bracken, 2005; Metsala, 1999).

Although we may not be sure which of these views is correct, we do know that vocabulary skills are central to early literacy. Research overwhelmingly supports the role of preschool vocabulary in later reading comprehension (NICHD Early Child Care Research Network, 2005; Storch & Whitehurst, 2002). Common sense says that having a good vocabulary and strong oral language skills is important for success in school. We also know that classroom interventions can be quite effective at improving children's oral communication skills (National Early Literacy Panel, 2009).

# THE PROBLEM WITH VOCABULARY AND ORAL LANGUAGE SKILLS

Conversational language skills are what most people think of when they think of oral language skills.

## Conversational Language Skills

Children who have oral language problems and who speak in ungrammatical sentences using limited vocabulary often have later reading problems (DeThorne, Petrill, Schatschneider, & Cutting, 2010; Scarborough, 1990). Unfortunately, many children come to preschool and kindergarten having had in their home fairly limited conversations with adults of the kind that promote language development (Hart & Risley, 1995). Interventions that focus on conversational skills can have a dramatic impact on the development of oral language (Ruston & Schwanenflugel, 2010). For this reason, conversational language skills are discussed in Chapter 2.

## Listening Comprehension Skills

Good listening comprehension skills during preschool are strong indicators of good reading comprehension later (Lynch et al., 2008; Verhoeven & van Leeuwe, 2008). One of the most common ways in which children develop good literacy-related listening skills is through adults reading to them. Adults who read storybooks to children have a profound impact on the children's development of listening comprehension skills. Experience with being read to has been directly linked to good general literacy and language development (Mol, Bus, & de Jong, 2009; Snow, Burns, & Griffin, 1999). Interactive reading, in which adults engage in open-ended, inference-inducing interactions while reading to children, is particularly beneficial for preschoolers (Beck & McKeown, 2001; Senechal, Thomas, & Monker, 1995; Whitehurst et al., 1994). Unfortunately, many families have remarkably limited access to children's books in their homes and neighborhoods (Neuman & Celano, 2001), making it difficult for extensive book reading to occur. We talk about how to implement effective storybook reading in the classroom in Chapter 3.

## Vocabulary Skills

Many children come to school lacking the vocabulary they need for early academic success. By the time they enter pre-K or kindergarten, their peers may already know several thousand more words than they do (Hart & Risley, 1995). These children are behind before they have even begun, having as much as a 1- or 2-year achievement gap in terms of vocabulary before they even enter first grade. Unless teachers intentionally focus on building vocabulary skills, the needs of these children may go unmet even in the best early childhood programs.

## THE *PAVEd FOR SUCCESS* PROGRAM

The *PAVEd for Success* program provides a set of classroom strategies and materials that focus on improving children's vocabulary and oral language skills. In our experience, teachers are often given pretty general advice regarding how to support the growth of children's vocabulary and oral language skills. Generally speaking, teachers are told to 1) talk more with children, 2) read books to children, and 3) target specific vocabulary. We have come to think of this advice for supporting vocabulary growth in terms of the three-legged stool depicted in Figure 1.1. We agree with this general advice but recognize that more clarity is needed regarding better and worse ways of carrying it out in the classroom. The *PAVEd for Success* program is designed to formalize this advice with effective practices that can be used in classrooms. In each chapter we explain in great detail classroom practices designed to help children develop vocabulary and oral language skills.

On the left-hand leg of the stool is the advice "Talk more." We describe what our research has shown to be effective ways of talking with children in Chapter 2, Building Bridges. On the middle leg is the advice "Read more." We describe recommended practices for reading books in Chapter 3, CAR Quest. Finally, on the right-hand leg is the advice "Teach vocabulary." We discuss how to select vocabulary and choose activities that support the learning of new vocabulary in Chapter 4, New VEhicles.

### Research Validation of *PAVEd for Success*

Since the early 2000s, we have been engaged in studies designed to evaluate the effectiveness of the *PAVEd for Success* program for developing vocabulary and oral language in pre-K and kindergarten children. We have taken a value-added approach to the development of the program. That is, our guiding question has been whether the addition of some practices is really worth it

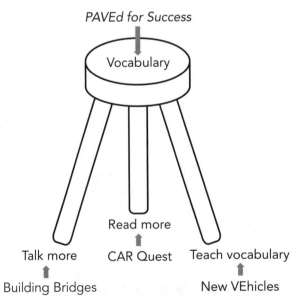

**Figure 1.1.**   Illustration depicting the organization of the *PAVEd for Success* program. Each leg of the vocabulary "stool" represents an element: Building Bridges (talk more), CAR Quest (read more), and New VEhicles (teach vocabulary).

in terms of producing growth in children compared with not having those practices. Are teachers able to carry out the program? This question is important because a program that does not work for teachers cannot possibly work for children. Our goal in developing *PAVEd for Success* was to provide teachers with research-based practices that could be adapted to their unique classroom structures and that built on their professional expertise. Furthermore, we are very aware of the many demands on teachers for the valuable "real estate" of the school day. So the practices we recommended had to be effective. We developed solutions to problems of program implementation based on input and feedback from teachers every step of the way.

We evaluated variations of the program in a major study carried out with pre-K teachers and children (Schwanenflugel et al., 2010). We considered some practices so central to children's literacy readiness that no credible preschool literacy program could be without them. These practices included an emphasis on storybook reading, teacher conversation, alphabet instruction, and a classroom environment rich in print. We provided all teachers in the experimental condition with professional development in these practices. Some teachers also received professional development in carrying out phonological awareness (PA) activities. Some other teachers, however, received professional development in explicit vocabulary enhancement (VE) strategies. Still others received training in all practices (PAVE). It all clicked—we're paving the road for our students' success, hence the name *PAVEd for Success.* The full pre-K *PAVEd for Success* program included CAR Quest, New VEhicles, Building Bridges, and code-related activities. We followed children and their teachers throughout the pre-K year and just the children into kindergarten.

By the end of the pre-K year, children in the pre-K *PAVEd for Success* program demonstrated better expressive vocabularies than did children in the control group who were enrolled in early childhood settings of similar quality. The *PAVEd for Success* children, who began the year well below the national average on standardized tests of expressive vocabulary (i.e., they entered school testing on average at the 32nd percentile), ended the year at the 47th percentile, quite close to the national average (i.e., the 50th percentile). Nonprogram children did not make nearly as much progress (i.e., they ended the year at the 37th percentile). Expressive vocabulary represents an important aspect of vocabulary knowledge—the ability to name and use vocabulary words. These impressive results suggested that all of the extra attention to vocabulary was indeed worth it.

Unique to the *PAVEd for Success* program, however, is its effect on early literacy skills directly related to reading, particularly for those children who had entered pre-K with very low levels of literacy skills and knowledge. Such children are vulnerable to reading difficulties and may need special reading services later on. By the end of kindergarten, the kindergarten Dynamic Indicators of Basic Early Literacy Skills (DIBELS; Good & Kaminski, 2002; Kaminski & Good, 1998), a widely used screener for early literacy problems, showed that, compared with children in a control group, fewer of these children were designated as needing substantial intervention. Furthermore, an early decoding test showed that, unlike children in the control group, they had already started to read a substantial number of simple words, a very good sign indeed. Given the stability of such skills across early elementary school (Juel, 1988), it is reasonable to assume that children who show an early ability to read will likely continue to develop those skills later! We knew we were on to something.

To develop a better program, we talked with teachers about the challenges they had using the program in their classroom. We observed successful teachers to identify classroom practices that worked. Most important, we listened to teachers' suggestions about how to improve the program. For example, teachers indicated that having to pull together the various New VEhicles components (i.e., the words, pictures, books, and activities) was too time consuming, although they saw the value in it. They suggested that we supply these things to teachers. When we did so in a subsequent federal study with Mississippi Delta region kindergartens (SERVE

Center, 2010), teachers did indeed use them to good effect. These classroom materials are supplied in the units provided with this program and on the accompanying CD-ROM.

The federal evaluation of the use of the *PAVEd for Success* program for kindergarten classrooms found positive impacts for children (Goodson, Wolf, Bell, Turner, & Finney, 2010). Like the pre-K study, the evaluation found that the program had positive impacts on expressive vocabulary. Also, because the link between vocabulary and general knowledge base is a strong one (DeMarie, Aloise-Young, Prideaux, Muransky-Doran, & Gerda, 2004), the program benefited the development of general academic knowledge by the end of the school year. Moreover, this increase in vocabulary skills and academic knowledge did not come at the expense of classroom time spent on other important literacy skills.

We saw that some teachers had difficulty keeping records and scheduling the many small groups associated with the program. We also saw that some teachers successfully solved these problems by having a more or less fixed schedule for the children that they used consistently from week to week. For example, for Building Bridges, one teacher displayed a master schedule for conversations using Talking Center and Eat with the Teacher days. Her children really looked forward to "their day." She was able to say, "Can you tell me about it at the Talking Center tomorrow? I can't wait to hear it!" and children saved up things to talk about with their teacher. Thus, we have included examples of typical schedules that can be adapted for other classrooms in Chapter 5.

We also learned that successful teachers connected their vocabulary activities with other aspects of the curriculum. With this in mind, we have designed the units to connect to common state preschool and kindergarten science and social studies standards (primarily) as well as national literacy standards. In fact, teachers in our Mississippi Delta study often commented that the units supplied with this program helped them carry out their science and social studies curricula. It allowed them to better understand how important literacy concepts can be integrated throughout the day.

## ORGANIZATION OF THE BOOK

In Chapters 2, 3, and 4 we present research-based evidence supporting each of the PAVE strategies and discuss how each component of the program can be implemented in a pre-K or kindergarten classroom. To further illustrate the importance of supporting the development of children's vocabulary and oral language skills, we introduce each of the chapters with a brief case example of an individual child's experiences. Steve is meant to be representative of the many children we have had in our early childhood classrooms. We characterize Steve as a child with somewhat less-competent language skills, living not in poverty but in a working-class family. Steve may not be the first child we think of when we think about children who have less than ideal language skills—he is not language delayed, nor is he receiving early intervention or special education services. He is simply a quiet child who, without the necessary support, is far too likely to fall behind. Fortunately for Steve, his teachers can make a difference. In the later chapters we discuss how teachers can integrate PAVE into their existing literacy program and class routines (Chapter 5), create their own vocabulary units if they so desire (Chapter 6), and use PAVE successfully with diverse learners (Chapter 7). Throughout the book we provide classroom examples to illustrate how different teachers use PAVE within their classrooms. We have drawn on many discussions with and observations of teachers in writing these classroom examples, and we appreciate how willingly teachers have shared their ideas with us.

*PAVEd for Success* is a program evaluated to have positive impacts on children's vocabularies, designed by and for preschool and kindergarten teachers. We hope you will find this program as beneficial as your peers have, and we thank you for your dedication to children.

# 2

---

# Building Bridges

## Conversations with Children that Build Vocabulary

**A**ll teachers have conversations with their students. They talk to them about all sorts of things during the course of the school day. Wouldn't it be wonderful if teachers could design these conversations so that they were not only discussing classroom goings-on but also building students' vocabulary significantly and, as a bonus, building caring relationships? *PAVEd for Success* does just that with its Building Bridges component. Just by tweaking their conversations with students, teachers can make a huge impact on students' language development (Girolametto, Weitzman, & Greenberg, 2006). The more teachers talk personally with students, and the more comfortable students feel initiating conversations with their teachers, the more improvements students will see in their oral language skills (Wells, 1986).

## CONVERSATIONS WITH CHILDREN THAT BUILD VOCABULARY

Often when teachers think about having conversations with their students, they think about all the talking they themselves do. Let's switch our perspective a bit and consider the language experience of a single child.

## Case Study _ _ _ _ _ _ _ _ _ _ _ _ _ _ _ _ _ _ _ _ _ _ _ _ _ _ _ _ _ _ _ _ _ _ _ _ _ _

Steve is a quiet child without the language skills of his classmates. During much of his day, Steve listens to his teacher tell the class as a group what they should be doing (Layzer, Goodson, & Moss, 1993). Approximately 30% of the talk he hears from his teacher is about daily routines and transitions: "Time for cleanup!" "Line up for recess!" "Please put your books in your baskets. We need to go to music!" (Dunn, Beach, & Kontos, 1994). Steve listens, follows directions, and does not draw his teacher's attention. Of course, his teacher does much more than give directions; she also introduces ideas, explains concepts, and clarifies confusing material. Steve listens and certainly learns from his teacher. He also learns by observing his classmates: About 10% of the time, he watches other, more verbally gifted children have animated conversations with his teacher (Layzer et al., 1993). Steve is learning by watching and listening. Is this enough for Steve? He loves his teacher and wants to go up and talk with her, but he is shy and has little experience starting up conversations with adults. As is the case with many children, conversation in his home is more or less limited to being told what to do (Hart & Risley, 1995). So even when his teacher is standing right next to him, he gets missed somehow (Wilcox-Herzog & Kontos, 1998). Despite his teacher's best intentions, he often goes home not having had any one-to-one time with his teacher all day, his language skills unchanged (Wells & Wells, 1984).

The Building Bridges component of this program is designed to help ameliorate this kind of problem by helping teachers have regular conversations. These conversations target specific vocabulary and oral language development skills and, as a bonus, might help develop more positive teacher–student relationships (Wilcox-Herzog & Kontos, 1998). The conversations in Table 2.1, which were taken from our program, illustrate just how quickly young children can pick up new words from an intentionally designed conversation with a teacher (Ruston & Schwanenflugel, 2010).

It is pretty obvious that Jonathan did not know the word *gargantuan* and Emil did not know the word *crunching* before these experiences. They may not remember their new words forever just from this one experience, but vocabulary learning is incremental: It moves from being unfamiliar to being kind of familiar to being understood and then becomes fully usable in children's own speech (Schwanenflugel, Stahl, & McFalls, 1997). The beauty of this approach is that all of this instruction occurred while the adult was simply carrying out a language-rich conversation. It might not feel like instruction, but we believe it is the most important vocabulary instruction that a teacher might do. This is how teachers build an oral language bridge. And that is why we call this strategy *Building Bridges*.

## IMPLEMENTING BUILDING BRIDGES IN THE CLASSROOM

Now that we have laid out the fundamental rationale for teachers to carry out small-group conversations with children, let us turn to how to implement this idea with some practicality into the classroom.

**Table 2.1.**   Examples of children learning new words from teacher conversation

Example 1

**Jonathan:** Bigger!

**Mr. Mac:** Bigger? What's another word for *big*? (Mr. Mac blows up a balloon.) Should I make it more *gargantuan*?

**Jonathan:** Yeah!

**Mr. Mac:** Even more *gargantuan*?

**Jonathan:** Make it *gargantuan*!

Example 2

**Ms. Maldo:** I heard *crunching*….

**Emil:** I hear a *crunch*.

**Ms. Maldo:** You heard a *crunch*? I heard a noise, a *crunching* noise….

**Emil:** *Crunching* up.

## How Much Time Does It Take?

Of course it is not practical to hold long one-to-one conversations with every child in the classroom, but working in small groups of up to five to seven children can serve a similar purpose (Dickinson, Cote, & Smith, 1993). Teachers only need to schedule 15 minutes a week for each group because our research suggests that this may be enough time to jump-start the development of vocabulary and oral language skills. Teachers have limited classroom time and are often asked to schedule many activities into their already crammed days. But Building Bridges is worth it. The relatively small amount of time spent on these conversations can lead to significant increases in children's vocabulary over time (Ruston & Schwanenflugel, 2010). And the 15 minutes of conversation does not have to happen all at once. In fact, many teachers have found that breaking the 15 minutes up into three 5-minute small-group conversations works best.

Here are some ideas for when to incorporate Building Bridges, as suggested by teachers:

- With early arrivals and late departures
- In ongoing dramatic play, art, and extension activities
- In daily hikes around the playground during recess
- During Eat with the Teacher day
- In a Talking Center designed specifically for holding conversations
- In follow-up activities to even up the timing across small groups

Whatever time you choose, it is important to have regularly scheduled, consistent, and predictable conversations so that children know when their special time to talk to their teacher is coming up. Children really look forward to these opportunities to talk to their teacher, so a public schedule such as the one shown in Figure 2.1 works best.

Every teacher has many time pressures. That's one good reason why it may be beneficial to use any and all of the adults in the classroom (e.g., assistant teachers, speech-language pathologists, parent or student volunteers) to carry out these Building Bridges groups. You can show them how to carry out these techniques in a fairly short period of time by modeling conversations for them. When other adults use these techniques, it will save you time and give children more opportunities to build their oral language skills.

| Time | Conversation | | | | |
|---|---|---|---|---|---|
| | Monday | Tuesday | Wednesday | Thursday | Friday |
| Meal | Shondra | D'Adrious | George | Stephanie | Sara |
| | Ezekiel | Isabella | Paul | Rebekah | Martin |
| | Emil | Fortuna | Willy | Melanie | Nicole |
| | Precious | Rebecca | Kim | William | Steven |
| | Tommy | Matthew | Eliza | Diana | Jeff |
| Snack | Sara | Stephanie | Shondra | D'Adrious | George |
| | Martin | Rebekah | Ezekiel | Isabella | Paul |
| | Nicole | Melanie | Emil | Fortuna | Willy |
| | Steven | William | Precious | Rebecca | Kim |
| | Jeff | Diana | Tommy | Matthew | Eliza |
| Talking Center | George | Sara | Stephanie | Shondra | D'Adrious |
| | Paul | Martin | Rebekah | Ezekiel | Isabella |
| | Willy | Nicole | Melanie | Emil | Fortuna |
| | Kim | Steven | William | Precious | Rebecca |
| | Eliza | Jeff | Diana | Tommy | Matthew |

**Figure 2.1.**   One teacher's schedule for Building Bridges conversations.

## How Do I Decide the Makeup of Each Group?

Of course all children should be comfortable enough with their group that they will feel free to talk. Here are some suggestions. Place the quiet children together. Talkative children with exceptional verbal skills are likely to take over in small groups. They can intimidate quiet, less verbal children, so grouping quieter children in small groups is recommended. Or place children together who have been identified as needing extra help through, for example, pre-enrollment screening. That way you may be able to give them extra conversation time to help them catch up. Practices in Building Bridges are especially beneficial to children who begin the year with limited vocabulary and linguistic skills (Ruston & Schwanenflugel, 2010).

## How Can I Keep Track of What's Happening?

We recommend that you maintain some sort of record-keeping system to ensure that the Building Bridges groups are being carried out. If a fixed schedule is set up at the beginning of the year, then there is little need to spend much time determining who has and who has not received the appropriate weekly Building Bridges conversations. You would just need to track absences to determine who has missed their groups. Appendix B provides a Student Tracking Tool that teachers can use, but of course you can choose whatever monitoring system works best in your classroom.

## What Do I Talk About and How?

Sometimes teachers find practicing Building Bridges conversations uncomfortable and unnatural at first. That's not surprising. Typically teachers do not focus on vocabulary building when they are having a conversation with someone. However, with continued practice the conversation guidelines we provide here will soon become second nature (see Table 2.2).

### Let the Children Select the Topic

Don't we all like to talk about our own interests? Of course! That's why letting students bring up their own topics while you weave in rich words related to their interests serves two purposes: First, the children feel you are genuinely interested in them and so are more motivated to have these conversations, and second, you give them words they will be more likely to use repeatedly because they relate to their interests. The units in Section II provide some conversation starters (Start 'em Up! Topics) for each of the vocabulary units in case children are initially reluctant to talk. In our experience this problem is very short-lived, and pretty soon children are saving up topics for their teacher. Generic topics such as family; parties; injuries; pets; and unusual objects such as wire whisks, spaghetti strainers, auto parts, and so forth always work. Many teachers have found that using old recycled cell phones as conversation props helps quiet children warm up.

**Table 2.2.**   Guidelines for implementing Building Bridges in the classroom

| |
| --- |
| Let the children select the topic. |
| Allow adequate wait time. |
| Listen with genuine interest. |
| Keep the conversation positive. |
| Encourage turn-taking among the children. |
| Hold linguistically complex conversations with young children. |

## Allow Adequate Wait Time

Young children, particularly those with poor linguistic skills, take longer to process their thoughts and may just need extra time to formulate a response. Slow down the pace a bit, particularly if a child is an English language learner (ELL) or has a language impairment.

## Listen with Genuine Interest

Teachers can show children that they are genuinely interested in what they have to say by their facial expressions. They can interject empathetic responses (e.g., "Really!" "Uh huh!" "No kidding!" "What happened next?"). They can ask for clarification. They can crouch down to the child's level. They can stay on the child's topic—listening to young boys' descriptions of their favorite superhero might not excite us as teachers, but it's interesting to them, so we must try to show interest nonetheless!

## Keep the Conversation Positive

Positive teacher–student relationships have long-term consequences for later schooling (Mashburn, Hamre, Downer, & Pianta, 2006). Over the years teachers have often told us how much they appreciate getting to know their students better through Building Bridges. Unconditional acceptance through positive Building Bridges conversations helps build these relationships (Howes, Hamilton, & Phillipsen, 1998). Teachers sometimes slip into academic talk, asking questions that have correct answers and focusing on topics related to academic competencies. Conversations framed around academic tasks are less positive for some children and may discourage them from talking.

## Encourage Turn-Taking Among the Children

Not only should children not interrupt one another but also they should stay on the topic at hand. Listening to others is a conversational skill. If a child changes the topic, the teacher should gently remind him or her about the ongoing topic unless it is a natural transition. Of course teachers need to model these skills themselves.

## Hold Linguistically Complex Conversations with Young Children

All talk is not equal in terms of encouraging the development of vocabulary. There needs to be some degree of linguistic complexity to these conversations. This is where teachers need some intentionality, because usually in classroom conversations they try to be clear and often simplify their talk. Keep the following in mind:

1. *Respond with alternative and more sophisticated words or, in linguistic terms, vocabulary recasts.* We like to think in terms of nickel words or dime words. Thus, if a child says, "She ain't got *no bike*," we might respond, "I wonder why there are *insufficient tricycles* for all of the children. I guess *tricycles* are *scarce* at this school." Both statements say pretty much the same thing, but one is a vocabulary recast of the other. The child uses the nickel words *no* and *bike*, whereas the teacher models the rarer dime words *insufficient*, *scarce*, and *tricycles* (see Table 2.3 for more examples). Children of this age (i.e., 3- to 5-year-olds) are less likely to use the following:

   a. Category words such as *furniture* or *musical instrument* (Gelman, Wilcox, & Clark, 1989)

   b. Specific words such as *robin, parakeet, waddle,* or *saunter* rather than *bird* or *walk* (Berlin, 1992)

**Table 2.3.** Examples of rare words for vocabulary recasts

| Nickel (typical) word | Dime (less commonly used) words |
|---|---|
| wet | soaked, drenched, damp, moist |
| happy | delighted, thrilled, ecstatic, content |
| look | peer, search, stare |
| car | sedan, convertible, SUV, vehicle |
| talk | converse, blab, chatter, gossip |
| run | sprint, trot, jog, race |

   c. Less typical items from common categories (e.g., *cranberry* and *mango* rather than *apple* or *banana*; Mervis, 1987)

   d. Words for values, feelings, and thoughts (e.g., *generosity, disgusted, joy, confuse;* Schwanenflugel, 1991)

Adults are surprisingly good judges of how rare words are (Balota, Milotti, & Cortese, 2001) and how old they themselves were when they learned those words (Auer & Bernstein, 2008; Gilhooly, 1984). We have seen that teachers are generally good judges of their students' vocabulary levels.

2. *Expand on what the children say.* Children may need your help to learn complex grammar and elaborated speech. Talk that is elaborated and complex helps children develop better vocabulary and oral language skills (Hoff-Ginsberg, 1990). Table 2.4 shows examples of sentence expansions from teachers. Sentence expansions show children what the grammar might look like for their sentence. They show them how to use more precise language and vocabulary such as *upper, elementary,* and *playscape.* They indicate that their teacher understands the children. All without overt corrections of the children's speech!

3. *Ask open-ended questions.* Open-ended questions cannot be answered with a single word. If a teacher asked, "How did you think that happened?" the child would have to answer using at least a single complete sentence. Open-ended questions that emphasize abstract reasoning (e.g., questions about reasons, people's intentions and feelings, and predictions; Curenton & Justice, 2004) are particularly helpful for vocabulary development. Some examples of open-ended questions can be found in Table 2.5.

Starting questions with the words *why* and *how* is just as effective as the old standby "Can you tell me more?" Try to avoid concrete and fill-in-the-blank questions (e.g., "The color of your shirt is what?") because they do not help with language growth. Practice creating your own vocabulary recasts, sentence expansions, and open-ended questions to follow up on the statements in Table 2.6, which we have actually heard children say.

**Table 2.4.** Examples of sentence expansions

**Shondra:** My sister Jennie 'dere.

**Mr. Mac:** Your sister Jennie is over there on the *upper elementary playscape*?

**Emil:** We got a trick or treat.

**Ms. Maldo:** You went trick or treating after school?

**Precious:** Pushing it down.

**Ms. Maldo:** Yeah, they're pushing it down. Yeah, she's pushing the balloon down.

**Table 2.5.**  Examples of open-ended questions

**Shondra:** Look at this!
**Mr. Mac:** Excellent! What can you tell me about it?

**Jonathan:** My mama car nasty.
**Mr. Mac:** Why do you think it is?

**Ms. Maldo:** Let's make a pond too. How would we make a pond?
**Emil:** It wet right there.

## What About Students Who Are English Language Learners and/or Those with Disabilities?

We talk more about meeting the needs of diverse learners in Chapter 7. But in terms of Building Bridges, we recommend some additional practices. It would make sense to reduce the Building Bridges group size to two or three children if possible. Sit side by side and show joint attention to something that the child is doing—a puzzle, a classroom manipulative, or a drawing. Free play, center time, recess, or mealtimes are ideal for this. Then talk or monologue about what the child is doing. Talk slowly and clearly with articulate, expressive pronunciation. Use gestures so that the child can begin to see how the speech maps onto the concrete environment. Ask questions, but be satisfied with one-word answers for a while. Carry out a linguistic expansion on those one-word answers using the child's words. *Really* increase wait time. You may wish to try to learn some words in the children's native language as a conversation starter.

## Will Building Bridges Make a Difference?

We know from our research that Building Bridges will lead to significant increases in children's vocabulary (Ruston & Schwanenflugel, 2010). We have also heard from teachers time and time again about the impact Building Bridges has had on individual students. One of the most consistent themes of our work with teachers regarding the Building Bridges component is how much better they have gotten to know their students than in previous years—and that may be reason enough to use it!

**Table 2.6.**  Examples of sentences from 4-year-olds

She ain't got no book.

I be a piwate in Halloween.

I got a eye patz on n'eye.

I Spiderman.

He done fix duh 'tove.

## Classroom Example

Ms. Cameron begins the day by introducing their new unit, Gardening. She looks at her Building Bridges schedule in the morning and identifies the group of children with whom she will be having her Building Bridges conversations (Tyree, Macy, Paul, Roberto, and Nancy) during work time. She selected these children to be in this particular group because they were all rather quiet souls and seemed to get along with one another. Her experience told her that they should be able to converse together amicably.

Later in the morning, she calls these children over to the science area that she has stocked with garden paraphernalia. Her plan is to start with a Building Bridges session followed by a vocabulary extension activity. She has another group of children working with her assistant and another working independently in a small group. Because this is a particularly shy group, she knows that her goal with this Building Bridges session is to get these children talking. She begins the conversation by recounting a story from her own life: "Last year, I planted cucumbers and radishes in my garden. I raked and hoed all the soil up first. Then I planted my seeds. I ended up with so many cucumbers that I gave all my neighbors some." Then she introduces the suggested Start 'em Up! Topic for this unit: "If you had a garden, what would you grow in it?"

Macy ventures, "Tomatoes?"

Tyree chimes in, "I put cucumbers."

"Really, Macy? You would plant tomatoes in your garden? Tyree, you want to plant cucumbers in your garden?" Ms. Cameron says, expanding her students' simple sentences. "Why would you plant tomatoes, Macy? Why cucumbers, Tyree?" She hopes these open-ended questions will induce more talk.

"I like tomatoes," says Macy. "My mama cut 'em up."

"I like 'em," says Tyree.

"So your mother *slices* them up and makes a lovely *feast* out of them? Do you ever help her make dinner, Macy?" Ms. Cameron says, trying to introduce some rare vocabulary into the conversation.

"Yes, I help. I can't slice though," Macy points out. Ms. Cameron is thrilled that Macy has used her word *slice*.

But Roberto chimes in, "I put plates."

"You put out the plates and *silverware*? You help your mother *set the table*? Good for you, Roberto! I'm sure that she greatly appreciates that." Ms. Cameron guesses, correctly, that, being an English language learner (ELL), Roberto is probably not familiar with the phrase *set the table*. She is happy he feels confident enough to jump into the conversation. She has kept the conversation positive to encourage that.

The conversation goes on like this, with each child describing how he or she helps at home. They start to talk about chores their siblings do at home and how maybe their siblings don't do all of the chores they are supposed to. She is happy that the conversation has drifted from gardens to house chores to siblings because the words she has introduced are more likely to be remembered if they relate to children's interests. Ms. Cameron asks open-ended questions, expands on children's statements, and adds in words the children are likely to be unfamiliar with until the 5 minutes are up. This Building Bridges session is over for now. She will meet with this group twice more this week.

Ms. Cameron then gets the children started on planting beans in moist plastic bags so that they can see the process of seed germination over the course of the week. They continue to talk, but now Ms. Cameron gently steers the conversation back to the topic of gardening.

CHAPTER

# 3

---

# CAR Quest

Storybooks are an important part of every early childhood classroom. Reading aloud shows children how books work and helps them learn about the world they live in, the print they see, and the words and language style used in books (Early Childhood-Head Start Task Force, 2002). But many teachers do not realize that the *way* in which they read to students—not just *what* they read—can make a huge difference in students' vocabulary and oral language skills. The CAR Quest component of *PAVEd for Success* enables teachers to structure their reading of storybooks in ways that have maximal impact on children's vocabulary and oral language skills. During the book discussion, teachers structure their interactions around books to reflect three different question levels: *C*ompetence, *A*bstract, and *R*elate.

## IMPLEMENTING CAR QUEST IN THE CLASSROOM

Reading books to students is one of the most pleasant and successful ways to launch them into literacy. Vocabulary in books tends to be different from the vocabulary used in everyday conversations; to improve the kind of vocabulary that students will later use as independent readers, it is important to read aloud to them. Yet no matter how good their intentions, teachers often get so caught up in daily minutiae and external pressures that they spend precious little time reading to students. In fact, observational studies of many early childhood programs show that children are read to less than 5 minutes a day (Dickinson et al., 2003) and that many students spend much more time during the school day washing their hands and transitioning between activities than listening to their teachers read books (Dickinson & Tabors, 2002)!

## Case Study _____

Consider, once again, Steve, the shy, quiet child whose language skills need bolstering. Because his parents have multiple jobs and other children, Steve is among the 30% of children nationally whose parents do not have time to read aloud, not even as much as once a week (Bradley, Corwyn, McAdoo, & Coll, 2001). His home has fewer than 15 children's books to choose from, and his neighborhood has neither a library nor a store that focuses on books for children (Neuman & Celano, 2001). He is lucky because his teacher recognizes the importance of reading books, but it is sometimes just a quick run-through at circle time in the morning. Steve does not say much during this reading, and the more verbally gifted children take over—again. Steve will learn lots about books during these read-alouds, but not nearly as much as he could.

It is not that Steve's teacher and early childhood teachers in general do not realize how important reading is. Of course they do! But unless they intentionally set aside time to read to students, the day flies by and before they know it, the students are going home. It is important for teachers to plan which books they will read and when they will read them during the course of the day. Reading a good book is a great transition tool—it is an easy and pleasant way to engage students at the start of the day, to move from one subject to another, to get them to settle down after lunch or recess, or to end the day. There are so many opportunities throughout the day if teachers consciously plan ahead for them. The CAR Quest read-aloud technique provides suggestions for incorporating more book-reading time into the classroom and increasing students' engagement during book reading (see Table 3.1).

## Read Each Book More than Once During the Week

Children love to hear the same story over and over again, and this is to their advantage. Children tend to miss key vocabulary and storylines on the first reading. Repeated readings of books help them with this. Research has shown that increasing the frequency of reading individual books leads to gains in children's vocabulary (Senechal, 1997). We recommend reading each book three times: twice as a large-group activity and once as a small-group activity.

Both large-group and small-group reading have their own benefits. Teachers use various kinds of talk during large-group times; they use talk to maintain and focus children's attention, to provide children with factual information, and to challenge them cognitively. Children's exposure to this kind of talk as preschoolers is positively related to their academic competence in kindergarten (Dickinson, 2001). Large-group read-alouds typically take place during whole-class activities such as morning meeting, circle time, or transition time. They are pretty flexible in that way.

The benefits of reading aloud, especially for students who are at risk for any reason, are amplified when reading occurs in a small-group setting (Whitehurst et al., 1994). This makes perfect sense. In a smaller group there are more opportunities for an individual child to interact with and talk about a book. Children's active participation in book-reading sessions actually doubles when they are read to as part of a small group compared with a whole class (Phillips & Twardosz, 2003). We recommend that children participate in a minimum of one large-group book reading per day and three small-group book readings per week. A small group consists of five to seven children. Even smaller groups are more effective for younger children, those who are ELLs, those with disabilities, and those who may need more enriched language experiences. These small-group read-alouds should include rereadings of books presented to the class in the large group.

We include some sample classroom schedules in Chapter 5 and some forms for keeping track of book-reading sessions in Appendix B. Keeping track of small-group book-reading sessions is important so that one can make sure that each child has ample opportunities to be involved in small-group book reading sessions. Conscious, intentional planning helps ensure that teachers will get the job done.

**Table 3.1.**   Guidelines for implementing CAR Quest in the classroom

Read each book more than once during the week.

Read books in both small- and large-group settings.

Introduce books by taking a "book walk."

Read the book interactively by using CAR Quest prompts.

Choose an additional topic-related book with good vocabulary.

## Introduce Books by Taking a "Book Walk"

Taking a book walk helps students think about what the book might be about, draws them into the story, and provides them with information before the teacher begins to read the text (Morrow, 2005). In a book walk the teacher introduces the book by showing the children the pictures and asking them what they think the book is about. The teacher also gives them a goal for listening.

Here is an example of how a teacher might approach a book walk for *When Sophie Gets Angry—Really, Really Angry…* (Bang, 1999), included in the Feelings unit. She begins the book walk by first showing the children the cover of the book and reading the title. The teacher then "walks" through the book, turning the pages and asking children for comments about the different pages: "What do you think is happening in this picture?" "How do you think Sophie feels?" The teacher helps them generate predictions about the story: "Sophie runs and runs and runs; where do you think she is running to?" "What do you think will happen when Sophie gets home?" The teacher then summarizes the main idea of the book: "This is a book about a little girl who gets very angry and what she does. While we're reading the book, let's think about why Sophie got angry and what she does to make herself feel better." A book walk will help children to think about the book before the teacher even begins reading the text.

## Read the Book Interactively by Using CAR Quest Prompts

Reading a storybook while asking questions engages students in the book-reading experience. The book becomes a stimulus for conversation. Moreover, asking questions while reading has a positive impact on vocabulary development in preschoolers (Beck & McKeown, 2001; Bus, van IJzendoorn, & Pellegrini, 1995; Dickinson & Smith, 1994; Valdez-Menchaca & Whitehurst, 1992; Wasik, Bond, & Hindman, 2006; Whitehurst et al., 1988). The *PAVEd for Success* vocabulary units provide a set of questions as a jumping-off point for this interactive reading. The three types of questions and the research-based purpose for each of them are shown in Table 3.2. We continue the metaphor of paving the road to success by using the acronym CAR to denote the three types of questions, which we call *CAR Quest prompts:* Competence, Abstract, and Relate.

### Competence Questions

Competence questions allow children to feel successful right from the start because they can find the information directly in the text or pictures of the storybook. They provide opportunities

**Table 3.2.**   Types of CAR Quest prompts

| CAR Quest prompt | What it does | Examples |
| --- | --- | --- |
| Competence | Allows children to demonstrate concepts they already know | What color is the boy's shirt in this picture?<br>Who is riding in that car? |
| Abstract | Requires children to infer information not immediately present in the story or pictures | What is the boy thinking?<br>How did that make him feel? |
| Relate | Encourages children to relate the information to their own experience | When was the last time you went somewhere in a car?<br>Did you do something special the last time it snowed? |

for students to be confident and comfortable in the book-reading interaction by demonstrating what they know (van Kleeck, 2003). They stimulate children's thinking about what is going on in the book and what the pictures tell them about the story. For example, when reading *When Sophie Gets Angry—Really, Really Angry...*, a teacher might ask, "Does Sophie look happy or sad in this picture?" or "What is Sophie doing here?"

## Abstract Questions

Abstract thinking questions are more challenging for young children. For example, when reading *When Sophie Gets Angry—Really, Really Angry...*, the teacher might ask, "Why do you think Sophie is disappointed?" "Why did Sophie's mother think her sister should have a turn?" "Where do you think Sophie will go when she feels better?" Research suggests that teachers support children's vocabulary growth by asking questions that are more challenging as well as those that are within their level of competence (van Kleeck, 2003). These abstract questions prompt children to make predictions, make inferences, and solve problems about the book; they challenge students to go beyond what is immediately in front of them in talking about the book so that they can truly understand what they are listening to. Why is this important? Because preschool and kindergarten children are unlikely to do this on their own (Lynch et al., 2008). They are unlikely to anticipate story events, imagine what characters are likely thinking, or determine the underlying causes of events in a story. It is important for teachers to guide them to do this because these kinds of inferences are the glue that holds stories together; without them, stories basically go misunderstood.

## Relate Questions

Relate questions ask children to relate the information in the book to their own personal experiences. Asking questions that bring children's prior knowledge to bear on a book is one of the most powerful tools teachers have in their arsenal to increase children's comprehension (Anderson & Pearson, 1984). For example, when reading *When Sophie Gets Angry—Really, Really Angry...*, the teacher might ask, "Have you ever been angry before? What happened?" or "Can you tell me about a time when you were disappointed about something?"

All of the *PAVEd for Success* vocabulary units suggest CAR Quest prompts for each of the books. We have generally found that asking six questions (i.e., two Competence, two Abstract, and two Relate) each time we are reading the book works well. We have indicated the page locations for each prompt by describing the relevant illustration so that teachers can easily locate the appropriate page for each prompt. Some teachers have found it helpful to write the prompts on sticky notes and attach the notes directly in the book to remind themselves when and where to ask the different types of questions.

Many teachers with whom we worked wondered whether the discussions generated by the CAR Quest prompts would take away from the story itself or whether the children would lose focus on the story and plot when the reading was interrupted by questions and discussion. These concerns are valid. The flow of the story is important to read-alouds, and asking too many questions will take away from the flow. Based on our experience in classrooms and based on teacher feedback, we have found that asking six questions provides the ideal balance between a lack of interaction and distracting levels of interaction.

## How to Choose Books to Read Aloud

Each of the *PAVEd for Success* vocabulary units lists two topic-related books for teachers to read over the course of the unit. Teachers can also include supplemental books as part of the unit. How did we choose these books? Some of the suggested books are fiction and some are informational books so that children learn to understand different kinds of books (Duke, 2004). Traditional storybooks and informational books differ on many levels (Price, van Kleeck, & Huberty, 2009). Informational books are designed to instruct about a particular knowledge domain; their vocabulary tends to be more domain specific and technical. Their structures are different: compare/contrast, cause/effect, problem/solution, description, or lists. By contrast, fiction is designed to entertain (Brewer & Lichtenstein, 1982). It has plots with settings, characters, problems, and resolutions; its vocabulary emphasizes cognitive and affective words. It is important for children to have experiences with both informational books and traditional literature. In Appendix A we discuss the alignment between PAVE and the Common Core State Standards for English Language Arts for kindergarten, which organize early literacy competencies separately for informational texts and traditional literature. When you choose books as you create your own units or supplement ours, try to include a mix of fiction and informational books.

## A Classroom Example

Ms. Woods begins each school day with a morning meeting with her kindergarten students. Today she is introducing a new book, *When Sophie Gets Angry—Really, Really Angry…*, which she will be reading as part of the Feelings unit. After the morning message and calendar, Ms. Woods introduces the book through a book walk by reading the title, showing the pictures, and asking the children about the illustrations. Ms. Woods summarizes by saying, "We'll be reading a book about a little girl who gets angry and what she does to feel better." Her first CAR Quest prompt is **Relate**: "Have you ever been angry before? What happened?" Lots of hands shoot up in the air, and some children begin to blurt out answers. Ms. Woods reminds children to raise their hands and calls on a couple of the children to hear their ideas. She tells the class that they will read this book again during morning work time and that everyone will have a chance to talk. Ms. Woods continues to read the book and engage children in further discussion using the remaining CAR Quest prompts included in the unit. She has found that sometimes, during the first reading of a book, discussions go a bit long, but she has planned for this and tries to encourage discussion. When she finishes the book she reminds children that they will all have a chance to read it again either later today or tomorrow. Ms. Woods does all of her large-group reading sessions during the morning meeting.

Later that morning during work time, Mr. Kaplan, a parent volunteer, comes in to help out. Ms. Woods does not always have parent volunteers, but this year she has been lucky. Mr. Kaplan comes in regularly on Mondays, and she can count on him to lead a small-group book-reading session. During the annual Pajama Storytime parent–teacher night, she demonstrated how to carry out read-alouds at home using CAR Quest reading strategies, so he is somewhat familiar with the routine. Ms. Woods writes the CAR Quest prompts on sticky notes for Mr. Kaplan and the other parent volunteers and attaches each note to the appropriate page of the book. This makes it easier for Mr. Kaplan to remember to ask the questions.

Today Ms. Woods notices that Mr. Kaplan's group is getting a bit noisy in their discussion; she is pleased with the discussion but makes a note to remember to talk with Mr. Kaplan about having the children use inside voices. As Mr. Kaplan finishes reading the book, he pulls out the bin she has provided with the supplies for making feeling collages, one of the extension activities included in the unit. Throughout the week Ms. Woods will rely on her teaching assistant to lead other small-group reading sessions.

# New VEhicles

## Explicit Vocabulary Enhancement Practices for Young Children

**W**e think children's development of vocabulary and oral language skills is best supported through a variety of intentional strategies. Children's road to literacy is *PAVEd for Success* by Building Bridges through extended conversations and by reading books interactively through CAR Quest. Teachers can also pave children's way to success and enhance their vocabulary by giving them word-learning skills or New VEhicles (Vocabulary Enhancement). The ultimate goal is not just to teach children specific sets of vocabulary words (though they will learn new vocabulary, of course) but, more important, to provide experiences that will enable them to become independent word learners.

## Case Study _ _ _ _ _ _ _ _ _ _ _ _ _ _ _ _ _ _ _ _ _ _ _ _ _ _ _ _ _ _ _ _ _ _ _ _ _ _ _ _ _ _ _ _ _ _

Consider, once again, Steve, the shy, quiet child with poorly developed language skills. By the time he was 3 there was already a sizeable vocabulary gap between him and his peers. He may only have acquired as little as *half* of the number of words of some of his peers (Hart & Risley, 1995). Luckily, Steve's parents sent him to community preschool, which helped him a little bit (McCartney, 1984). Steve still has trouble communicating his thoughts to his teacher and uses a lot of empty words and phrases such as "stuff," "that thing," and "over there." His teacher knows that unless something is done, by fifth grade Steve may end up as much as 3 years behind his peers in terms of vocabulary development (Biemiller, 2001). He will have trouble understanding what he is reading and communicating effectively. His teacher knows that among other things she must teach him some new words, but she does not know which words to teach him or how to go about doing it. For obvious reasons, dictionaries are out of the question.

Our focus in this chapter is on the strategies teachers use to introduce and reinforce children's learning of new vocabulary words; these are the New VEhicles. Guidelines for implementing New VEhicles in the classroom appear in Table 4.1. We begin with how to introduce new vocabulary words.

**Table 4.1.**   Guidelines for implementing New VEhicles in the classroom

Introduce new vocabulary words using Novel Name–Nameless Category (N3C).

Provide quick definitions.

Review new vocabulary words daily with picture cards.

Read topic-related books with embedded vocabulary using CAR Quest.

Reinforce the learning of new vocabulary with extension activities.

Post the vocabulary list.

Share new vocabulary words and unit topics with families.

## Introduce New Vocabulary Words Using Novel Name–Nameless Category

Young children—even toddlers—typically use a variety of ways to quickly connect new words to objects and events in their world (called *fast mapping*). This is how young children seem to be able to learn so many new words in such a short period of time. Many of the routines and activities in classrooms support children's learning in this way by connecting new words to objects or pictures. The picture books teachers read connect unfamiliar vocabulary with illustrations. The small vehicle sets, figures, or buildings in the block area are props children use to understand new words such as *ambulance, astronaut*, or *silo*. Similarly, dress-up clothes or props in the dramatic play area build on children's exploration and use of new words such as *stethoscope, colander*, or *helmet*. When teachers use props intentionally as a way to introduce new vocabulary, children seem to latch on to the meaning of these new words more quickly (Wasik & Bond, 2001; Wasik et al., 2006). In our research we have found that it is not just the use of props alone but how teachers use props or pictures to introduce new words that leads to real gains in children's vocabulary (Schwanenflugel et al., 2010). Children learn new words more quickly when teachers introduce these new words using the Novel Name–Nameless Category (N3C) strategy (Golinkoff, Mervis, & Hirsh-Pasek, 1994).

This strategy is easiest to understand by example. In Figure 4.1 there are three pictures: an apple, a banana, and a pickax. It is fair to assume that most children would be familiar with and able to name the apple and the banana. These are known vocabulary words. By contrast, most children will not know or be familiar with the pickax, a new vocabulary word introduced in the Fire Safety unit. If children are shown these three pictures and asked, "Which one is *pickax?*" they will use the N3C strategy to correctly identify the unknown object as the pickax. That is, they will quickly map this new vocabulary word (i.e., novel name) *pickax* to the unknown object (i.e., nameless category) in this set of pictures. The nice thing about introducing new words this way is that as long as the children are familiar with the known pictures, they will always have success in carrying out this exercise. It is a very basic guessing game that they will always get correct because they already have this strategy in their word-learning arsenal. The success children experience with this strategy makes learning vocabulary fun. For each of the vocabulary units, teachers will find a list of 10 new or unfamiliar vocabulary words related to the unit theme as well as paired known words to use in the N3C activity. We have developed a full set of picture cards for both the unfamiliar vocabulary words and the known words to use in the N3C activity, which are available on the accompanying CD-ROM.

The best time to use the N3C strategy is when introducing the unit topic. Most teachers find it easy to do this as part of a large-group morning meeting or circle time. As they introduce the new unit topic at the beginning of the week, they can begin by telling children, "We're going to thinking about fire safety, and we'll be learning some new words. Let's see if you can figure out which pictures match the new words." Then they introduce each of the 10 new vocabulary

**Figure 4.1.** Example of the Novel Name–Nameless Category (N3C) strategy. A teacher would expect that children would know *apple* and *banana*, whereas *pickax* may be unfamiliar. If children are asked which picture is the *pickax*, they will pick the unknown picture and correctly identify the new vocabulary word.

words using N3C. They show the picture card for each new vocabulary word with the picture cards for two known words. As they present the cards (e.g., for the words *hose*, *sock*, and *eye*), they simply ask, "Which one is *hose?*" Children will automatically connect the new word *hose* with the picture of the hose because they already know the terms for the pictures of the sock and eye.

Some teachers supplement the picture cards with props or objects they have in their classrooms; this can be especially helpful for younger children or ELLs. Using objects can be a great idea, but finding the right object to represent each vocabulary word can sometimes be difficult. In the Fire Safety unit, two of the new vocabulary words are *helmet* and *smoke*. Finding a helmet would be fairly easy (there is probably already one in the classroom's box of dress-up clothes); however, finding an object to represent smoke may be more challenging. This is why we have provided pictures for each of the words.

## Provide Quick Definitions

N3C helps children quickly grab hold of the new word, but children also need to understand the basic meaning of the word. Quick definitions provide simple explanations of each new vocabulary word. Quick definitions are designed to be kid-friendly, nontechnical definitions that give the basic essence of each vocabulary word's meaning. The quick definition for *pickax* is "Something you use to chop something down." This definition reflects how the word is used in the Fire Safety unit. Of course words sometimes have more than one meaning. For example, *gum* is a new vocabulary word included in the Dental Health unit. The quick definition we provide is "The pink stuff in your mouth that holds your teeth" rather than a definition related to chewing gum. Thus, our definitions are not designed to provide every meaning of the word—just the one related to the unit topic. Another feature of quick definitions is that they use simple terms to describe the new vocabulary, avoiding a common problem with dictionary definitions, which often contain too much unfamiliar vocabulary (Miller & Gildea, 1987).

Teachers get more mileage (forgive the pun) if they use quick definitions as they talk about the new vocabulary words in other settings and during the daily review of the new vocabulary. In our experience teachers have been successful using quick definitions immediately following the introduction of each word during the N3C, during the whole-group review of vocabulary with picture cards, or during the reading of the books following the mention of each vocabulary word within the text.

## Review New Vocabulary Words Daily with Picture Cards

Picture vocabulary cards can give children more practice with the new word to help them fully understand it and use it in their speech. It is important to show these cards to students each day and question the children about the vocabulary words. For example, the teacher could display all or some of the vocabulary picture cards and say, "Which one is _____?" Or later in the week he or she could simply point to each vocabulary picture card and ask for the appropriate label. Often it is easiest to do a quick vocabulary review before large-group reading.

Some teachers we have worked with have found it helpful to create a vocabulary word board with the picture cards. Some have attached a magnet to the back of each card and displayed the cards on a dry erase board or attached them using Velcro tape to a flannel board. Others have hung the pictures with clothespins from a clothesline. Some have simply tacked the picture cards to a bulletin board or easel or just propped them up on the eraser ledge of their chalkboard. Teachers can also use the picture cards to review the vocabulary as part of a game or small-group extension activity—vocabulary bingo cards are relatively easy to make, picture cards could be used as a treasure hunt to find a matching object in the classroom, or the picture cards could simply be available in a book corner along with related books.

## Read Topic-Related Books with Embedded Vocabulary Using CAR Quest

N3C is a good way to introduce new vocabulary, but for children to really "own" new words they will need lots of opportunities to hear and use these words for themselves. One way to give them this is through repeated CAR Quest readings of topic-related books (discussed in Chapter 3). Two trade books are included in each unit. In the Fire Safety unit, the two books are *Clifford the Firehouse Dog* (a storybook; Bridwell, 2005) and *Firefighters A to Z* (an informational book; Demarest, 2001). A teacher implementing New VEhicles might read *Clifford the Firehouse Dog* on Monday and Tuesday and *Firefighters A to Z* on Wednesday and Thursday, then choose a different book related to the unit topic to read on Friday. If teachers follow the CAR Quest approach, children will have lots of opportunities to hear the new vocabulary words as they reread the books in small and large groups and use their new words through CAR Quest prompts. As teachers read the books they can use quick definitions to reinforce word meanings.

One of the strategies we learned from teachers and incorporated into PAVE is *thumbs up/hands up;* this is an excellent way to keep children focused on the target vocabulary. In thumbs up/hands up children give a thumbs up when they hear one of the week's vocabulary words being read in the story. They give a hands up when they hear one of the vocabulary words introduced in earlier weeks. This strategy lets even less verbal children participate.

## Reinforce the Learning of New Vocabulary with Extension Activities

The more experience children have with new vocabulary words, the better their learning. This is why we have provided extension activities to use as you see fit. Each of the units includes three or four extension activities related to the unit topic. These activities can be used during centers or free play, as part of small-group work time, or as part of a science or social studies block. To derive maximum benefit each child should participate in at least two of the extension activities each week.

Extension activities provide children with more opportunities to practice their new words in different settings. For the Fire Safety unit, the extension activities include playing firefighter dress-up in the dramatic play area; making smoke detectors as an art project that can then be taken home to reinforce the vocabulary during family discussions; singing *I'm a Firefighter;* and practicing stop, drop, and roll. Teachers can also develop other activities related to the topic or incorporate lesson plans from other curriculum resources.

Teachers have found it helpful to put their own personal stamp on the program by figuring out how to embed PAVE into their own classroom routines. Some teachers have developed vocabulary show and tell, in which they ask children to bring in items from home or pictures they have drawn at home that illustrate one of the target vocabulary words. Other teachers have added a vocabulary center to their classroom by including a small two-person table, a three-ring binder for each child, writing utensils, and vocabulary pictures and labels. Children are encouraged to illustrate or write the new target vocabulary words and add them to their vocabulary binder. Finding ways to encourage vocabulary uses that fit within other classroom routines is a great idea!

## Post the Vocabulary List

The *PAVEd for Success* program is most effective when all of the adults in the classroom use the new vocabulary words with the children as often as possible. Prominently displaying each week's new vocabulary words is a good reminder for teachers, assistants, and other adults in the classroom.

## Share New Vocabulary Words and Unit Topics with Families

For each of the units, teachers will find a sample letter to send home to families so that new vocabulary words and unit topics can be shared at home. Feel free to simply copy this letter, or include this information in your usual form of parent communication. What is important is to let families know which new words children are learning so that they can use these words at home, as well. Teachers should give children as many opportunities as possible to use their new words both inside and outside of the classroom.

## A Classroom Example

Ms. Silva's preschool class will be exploring fire safety this week. On Monday she gathers the children on the rug for circle time. She begins by telling the children that they will be thinking about fire safety and points out some of the changes in the classroom—firefighter dress-up clothes and props have been added to the dramatic play area; fire trucks, sirens, and hydrants are now in the block area; several books on firefighters and fire safety are displayed in the book corner; and the sensory tub includes several hoses, small spray bottles with nozzles, and cups. As Ms. Silva highlights the changes, she can already see that the children are excited. She tells the children that they will be learning some new words related to fire safety. Then she introduces the new vocabulary words with N3C, showing each new vocabulary picture card with two known picture cards. She shows cards for *hose, sock,* and *eye.* The children ooh and aah over the pictures. Ms. Silva says, "Which one is *hose,* do you think?" As the children guess the right picture she provides the quick definition and then moves the picture card to the vocabulary wall. (She has placed a Velcro sticker on the back of each card and is using a flannel board as her vocabulary wall.) She presents the rest of the new vocabulary for the unit in this same way.

Ms. Silva then does a book walk to help children think about *Clifford the Firehouse Dog* and follows up by reading the book using the CAR Quest prompts. Later, children will explore and use their new vocabulary words during free play: Various centers are available for independent play, and Ms. Silva will reread *Clifford the Firehouse Dog* to a small group of children before they begin making their smoke detectors in the art area. She will use the Building

Bridges Start 'em Up! Topics to start her conversations with this small group while the children are cutting out, drawing, and gluing.

Ms. Silva will send the parent letter home at the end of the day with the children's smoke detectors along with a note asking parents to help the children do a safety check. Before lunch the children learn the *I'm a Firefighter* song, and out on the playground they will practice stop, drop, and roll. Finally, she has arranged for two local firefighters to bring in some of their equipment later in the week and talk about fire safety.

# 5
- - -

# Putting It All Together

Up to this point we have discussed each aspect of the program without putting them together as teachers might in their own classroom. In this chapter we look at how teachers put PAVE into action. Let's begin with the big picture.

As we explained in Chapter 1, we view oral language and vocabulary skills as only part of a high-quality literacy program. Code-based aspects of literacy—print and phonological awareness, letter knowledge, phonological decoding, and emergent writing—are very important but are not included in the *PAVEd for Success* program. Why? Because most early literacy programs already do a good job with these code-based areas. (We include an annotated list of suggested readings related to code-related skills in Appendix B.) However, when it comes to vocabulary and oral language skills, most programs are lacking. We have found that most literacy programs used in prekindergarten (pre-K) and kindergarten classrooms do not pay sufficient attention to vocabulary and oral language development, a fact that spurred us to develop PAVE. It is important to target both code-related and oral language–related skills in the early childhood curriculum. *PAVEd for Success* enhances rather than replaces most existing literacy programs. It would be difficult to imagine an early childhood classroom in which teachers did not read books, explain new words, or talk to children. In PAVE we have identified ways in which teachers can more intentionally focus on vocabulary and oral language skills within activities that are already part of their classrooms. We have organized these activities as topic-focused vocabulary units.

Think for a moment about how teachers can best teach vocabulary. They would probably start by identifying words that are going to be useful to children and ones that children will encounter in conversations or later as independent readers. Consider this simple list of five words: *calendar*, *calf*, *claws*, *carpenter*, and *cucumber*. These words are introduced in different PAVE units (Hooray for School!, Animal Babies, Bug Helpers, Careers and Community Helpers, and Gardening, respectively). Over the course of a year, children are likely to hear these words, perhaps as their teacher reads a book, as part of an exploratory science lesson, or through conversations (either in the classroom or at home). These words would be unlikely to appear in texts used as part of a literacy program focused on code-based skills or leveled readers. Some children will learn these words after only a brief exposure, but without an intentional focus, many will not. In terms of how best to teach new vocabulary, it would make little sense to teach this list of words. By contrast, a teacher could introduce a set of vocabulary words (e.g., *hygienist*, *braces*, *cavity*, *saliva*, and *x ray*) that relate to one another in a meaningful way (as they are used in the Dental Health unit). The teacher can then teach these words by introducing and defining them, reading and talking about books that include them, and engaging in classroom activities in which children use and practice them. This is why we have organized the vocabulary units around topics or themes.

The vocabulary units in Section II are resources; there is no prescribed order in which they should be presented, nor are you limited to using only these units (see Chapter 6 for guidance in creating your own unit). Most published early literacy programs are organized around familiar topics commonly found in early childhood classrooms (e.g., community helpers, feelings, seasons, weather). These topics are included in the PAVE units, and many teachers find that these vocabulary units can be aligned with topics already included in their current literacy program. Because it takes considerable practice for children to successfully develop vocabulary and oral language skills, we recommend emphasizing vocabulary across the curriculum. Some successful teachers who have carried out this program have chosen to align their vocabulary instruction with other curricular goals such as science, social studies, music, and art. Our work with pre-K and kindergarten teachers suggests that science and social studies in particular offer rich opportunities for vocabulary and language development. Because the PAVE units reflect common topics related to science and social studies, they provide an easy way to carry vocabulary learning across these other curriculum areas. In fact, many teachers use the PAVE units as a focus for teaching science and social studies, supplementing the PAVE activities with additional resources from their exploratory science kits or social studies texts. All of the PAVE units align with national science and social studies standards (see Appendix A).

Pre-K programs are less likely than kindergarten classrooms to use a standard literacy program. Instead these programs may follow a more general curricular model or approach. We have worked with pre-K and kindergarten teachers who use a variety of curriculum approaches. We have evaluated *PAVEd for Success* in pre-K classrooms using *The Creative Curriculum for Preschool, 4th Ed.* (Dodge et al., 2002), *HighScope* (Hohman, Weikart, & Epstein, 2008), and Montessori teaching approaches and in kindergarten classrooms using literacy programs such as *Open Court Reading* (McGraw Hill), *Success for All* (Success for All), and *Trophies* (Harcourt). All of these teachers were effective at integrating PAVE regardless of their curricular approach. In Appendix A we provide the learning standards for *The Creative Curriculum* and *HighScope* and the Head Start Child Development and Early Learning Framework to show how *PAVEd for Success* meets the standards of these different teaching approaches.

Many publishers of elementary reading series now offer thematically organized early childhood curricula for pre-K and kindergarten. These early childhood series often embed early literacy in an integrated or thematic approach to be used across content areas and throughout the day. Packaged curricula include typical daily schedules, specific trade books or anthologies, vocabulary lists, lesson plans across subject areas (or centers), and support materials to be used throughout the day. *Success for All* is perhaps the most recognized in terms of a comprehensive approach. Teachers in schools that have adopted *Success for All*, other thematic literacy curricula, or scripted approaches for literacy wonder how they can fit PAVE into their classroom. In response we can only share the advice offered by Dr. Lesley Mandel Morrow, a leading authority on early literacy and former president of the International Reading Association:

We have not found one published program that will determine the success or failure of literacy development with all young children. It is how you use the materials along with your basic philosophy and organization of the entire literacy program that will determine success.... As a teacher you must decide on the design of your literacy instruction, the materials you use, and how you use them. (2005, p. 150)

## How Do I Begin?

As teachers begin to implement PAVE in the classroom, they will need to consider how to introduce PAVE activities into their daily schedule, how to ensure that they are incorporating the various PAVE elements, how to support other classroom staff and volunteers in implementing PAVE, and how to involve families and to consider how they can assess student progress. We begin with scheduling.

## How Can I Schedule PAVE?

Early childhood programs use many different approaches to scheduling. In some classrooms, especially those serving younger children, children spend much of their day in free play or choice times, with perhaps two or three scheduled large-group times for circle or meeting. In programs serving older children, particularly kindergartners, children's time in free play typically decreases and their time in large group, organized small groups, and independent seat work increases (Dickinson, 2001). Schedules for PAVE activities should reflect the scheduling patterns already used in the classroom. Almost all early childhood programs bring children together for some period of large-group time, typically for storybook reading. CAR Quest interactive reading and New VEhicles vocabulary introduction and review can easily be added to an already existing circle or meeting time. Ensuring that all children participate in the small-group book-reading sessions and Building Bridges conversation groups can be the most challenging aspect of scheduling.

In programs that include large blocks of free play or choice time, such as those that use *The Creative Curriculum* or *HighScope*, teachers found it easiest to plan PAVE activities as centers or choice activities. For example, we have seen teachers create a Teacher Talk center. During free play a teacher remains in the Teacher Talk area, typically a cozy area with pillows or a rocking chair, and invites children to share conversations. Another idea is to schedule an adult to facilitate PAVE small-group sessions within the existing free choice centers. A teacher can be designated as the Building Bridges leader or storybook reader for a period during free play. Small-group Building Bridges conversations would then occur as part of children's activities in other centers and small-group book reading would take place as the teacher invites children into the book nook. Figure 5.1 shows how a teacher could schedule PAVE activities as part of a play-based curriculum.

Teachers who use a child-centered approach need to carefully monitor or track children's participation. We include a tracking tool in Appendix B for this purpose. As teachers engage a child in a particular activity, they note participation on the tracking tool. A daily review of the tracking tool will indicate which children did or did not participate, and teachers could follow up the next day by more intentionally focusing on having conversations with particular children or inviting reluctant readers into the book area. Remember that neither Building Bridges conversations nor small-group book reading has to occur during free play time. Either or both can be built into daily transitions—small-group reading with children who wake up early from nap, Building Bridges conversations during mealtime or snack. Teachers could approach the sched-

| 20 minutes | Circle time | Introduction or review of new vocabulary CAR Quest reading | |
|---|---|---|---|
| 90 minutes | Morning free play/centers | During free play/centers, all centers (art, blocks, dramatic play, manipulatives, sensory table) are open. The vocabulary extension activity is included in one of the centers. The teacher and assistant teacher conduct Building Bridges conversations as they interact with children in the centers. | |
| | | Approximately 10–20 minutes | CAR Quest: The teacher or assistant teacher remains in book area |
| | | Approximately 10–20 minutes | CAR Quest: The teacher or assistant teacher remains in book area |
| 90 minutes | Afternoon free play/ centers | Approximately 10–20 minutes | CAR Quest: The teacher or assistant teacher remains in book area |

**Figure 5.1.**   Sample daily classroom schedule for classrooms with an assistant teacher (child-centered approach). This schedule is useful for centers that use a more child-centered approach to scheduling. Both morning and afternoon free play or center time is included.

uling of vocabulary extension activities in a similar manner by leading one of the activities in the art, block, or dramatic play area and monitoring children's participation.

Teachers in public school pre-K and kindergarten classrooms typically have less flexibility over their classroom schedule than do early childhood educators working in non–public school settings. The overall school schedule dictates when the class as a group may leave for aesthetics or specials (art, music, or physical education), and when smaller groups or individual children are removed from the classroom to receive early intervention, special education, or English language services. There may be mandated blocks of time in which teachers are expected to teach literacy and mathematics. Depending on the literacy program being used, there may even be a schedule within the literacy block identifying how many minutes are to be devoted to whole-group instruction, small-group instruction, and independent seat work. Given these scheduling constraints, teachers can most effectively provide children with the sufficient number of small-group Building Bridges conversations, CAR Quest sessions, and extension activities by grouping children and scheduling individual groups. Many of the kindergarten teachers we have worked with schedule small-group sessions as part of their literacy block. As the teacher provides targeted small-group instruction related to the literacy program, an assistant teacher engages children in small-group reading sessions, Building Bridges conversations, or a vocabulary-related extension activity. We include a sample schedule based on this approach in Figure 5.2. Children can complete many of the extension activities included in the vocabulary units independently. However, having an adult facilitate discussion would better support children's vocabulary and oral language development. This is why we suggest that teachers carry the vocabulary focus into different content areas and schedule extension activities during a science or social studies block. Remember that small-group reading and Building Bridges sessions can also be scheduled during less structured instructional times, such as when children arrive in the morning, during morning snack, and before and after rest time.

The sample schedule in Figure 5.2 assumes the presence of an assistant teacher or some other adult volunteer in the classroom. Unfortunately, some teachers have limited support staff or none at all. Can PAVE be implemented in these classrooms? Yes, teachers have done this! The most successful approach involves embedding Building Bridges and CAR Quest small-group sessions into daily classroom routines. For example, as all of the children eat a snack, the teacher

| 20 minutes | Circle time | Whole class/ large group | | | |
|---|---|---|---|---|---|
| | | Introduction or review of vocabulary | CAR Quest reading | Literacy program activities | |
| 60 minutes | Literacy block | **Monday Small Groups** | | | |
| | | Assistant teacher | Teacher | Independent groups (or Adult volunteer) | |
| | 20 minutes | Building Bridges/ CAR Quest: Group 1 | Literacy program instruction: Group 3 | Vocabulary extension activity: Group 2 | Literacy program activity: Group 4 |
| | 20 minutes | Building Bridges/ CAR Quest: Group 3 | Literacy program instruction: Group 1 | (Optional) Group 4 | Literacy program activity: Group 2 |
| | 20 minutes | Building Bridges/ CAR Quest: Group 4 | Literacy program instruction: Group 2 | (Optional) Group 1 | Literacy program activity: Group 3 |
| 60 minutes | Literacy block | **Tuesday Small groups** | | | |
| | | Assistant teacher | Teacher | Independent groups (or adult volunteer) | |
| | 20 minutes | Building Bridges/ CAR Quest: Group 2 | Literacy program instruction: Group 4 | Vocabulary extension activity: Group 1 | Vocabulary extension activity: Group 3 |
| | 20 minutes | (Optional) Group 4 | Literacy program instruction: Group 1 | Vocabulary extension activity: Group 3 | Literacy program activity: Group 2 |
| | 20 minutes | Building Bridges/ CAR Quest: Group 4 | Literacy program instruction: Group 2 | (Optional) Group 3 | Literacy program activity: Group 1 |
| 60 minutes | Literacy block | **Wednesday Small groups** | | | |
| | | Assistant teacher | Teacher | Independent groups (or adult volunteer) | |
| | 20 minutes | Building Bridges/ CAR Quest: Group 1 | Literacy program instruction: Group 3 | Vocabulary extension activity: Group 2 | Literacy program activity: Group 4 |
| | 20 minutes | Building Bridges/ CAR Quest: Group 3 | Literacy program instruction: Group 1 | Vocabulary extension activity: Group 4 | Literacy program activity: Group 2 |
| | 20 minutes | (Optional) Group 4 | Literacy program instruction: Group 2 | (Optional) Group 3 | Literacy program activity: Group 1 |
| 60 minutes | Literacy block | **Thursday Small groups** | | | |
| | | Assistant teacher | Teacher | Independent groups (or adult volunteer) | |
| | 20 minutes | Building Bridges/ CAR Quest: Group 1 | Literacy program instruction: Group 3 | (Optional) Group 2 | Literacy program activity: Group 4 |
| | 20 minutes | Building Bridges/ CAR Quest: Group 2 | Literacy program instruction: Group 1 | (Optional) Group 4 | Literacy program activity: Group 3 |

**Figure 5.2.**    Sample weekly classroom schedule for classrooms with an assistant teacher (small-group approach). This schedule may be useful for teachers implementing PAVE within a literacy block. *Literacy program* refers to the required school literacy program designed to teach the full range of literacy skills.

*(continued)*

**Figure 5.2.**   *(continued)*

| 60 minutes | Literacy block | Thursday Small groups | | | |
|---|---|---|---|---|---|
| | | Assistant teacher | Teacher | Independent groups (or adult volunteer) | |
| | 20 minutes | Building Bridges/ CAR Quest: Group 4 | Literacy program instruction: Group 2 | Vocabulary extension activity: Group 3 | Literacy program activity: Group 1 |
| 60 minutes | Literacy block | Friday Small groups | | | |
| | | Assistant teacher | Teacher | Independent groups (or adult volunteer) | |
| | 20 minutes | Building Bridges/ CAR Quest: Group 2 | Literacy program instruction: Group 3 | Vocabulary extension activity: Group 1 | Literacy program activity: Group 4 |
| | 20 minutes | (Optional) Group 4 | Literacy program instruction: Group 1 | (Optional) Group 2 | Literacy program activity: Group 3 |
| | 20 minutes | Building Bridges/ CAR Quest: Group 3 | Literacy program instruction: Group 2 | Vocabulary extension activity: Group 4 | Literacy program activity: Group 1 |

reads a story and then conducts a Building Bridges session with a small group of children. Later in the day (perhaps during rest time, choice time, or even recess), the teacher again conducts these activities with a small group. A sample schedule for this approach is shown in Figure 5.3.

## How Do I Get Started?

Reading about something is quite different from actually implementing it in the classroom with students. Teachers have often found that it is helpful to practice Building Bridges and CAR Quest with another adult before moving on to full-scale implementation in the classroom. A few practice sessions are generally all that are needed. Copying the CAR Quest prompts onto sticky notes and posting them on the appropriate pages in the books is also very useful during start-up. Most teachers will implement New VEhicles as part of an existing morning meeting or circle time. As with anything new that is added to a large-group time, children will need to learn the routine. The first few times children are introduced to new vocabulary with N3C or review new vocabulary with picture cards, they may be hesitant to respond and uncertain of the routine. As they become more familiar with these practices, this routine will become smoother and less time intensive.

It is important to provide all children with the support they need in developing vocabulary and oral language skills. Monitoring and keeping track of individual children's participation in the various PAVE activities is critical. In Appendix B we include a simple tracking tool

| Activity | Monday | Tuesday | Wednesday | Thursday | Friday |
|---|---|---|---|---|---|
| Arrival/meal/snack | Group 1 | Group 2 | Group 3 | Group 1 | Group 2 |
| Rest time/recess/ choice time | Group 3 | Group 1 | Group 2 | Group 3 | Make-up time |

**Figure 5.3.**   Sample weekly classroom schedule for classrooms without an assistant teacher.

that many teachers have found useful. Some teachers may already have a system that works in their classroom—pocket charts, sticky note charts, or even popsicle sticks that they move into labeled cans. Teachers can use any system, but they do need to have a formal way to monitor children's participation. In Appendix B we also include a Teacher Checklist. At the conclusion of a vocabulary unit, teachers can use this checklist to reflect on how well the unit worked in terms of scheduling children's participation in the required number of small-group sessions, as well as the quality of the experiences (e.g., Were conversations linguistically complex? Were all of the CAR Quest prompts included in book reading?). Completing this form will allow teachers to consider areas in need of improvement and possible changes needed in their classroom practices. Of course there will be times—perhaps during a shortened school week due to vacations or in the absence of staff members—when not all PAVE activities will be included. This is understandable, but reviewing the checklists over time will both remind teachers of what needs to happen and highlight emerging patterns that need to be addressed.

## How Can I Mobilize Support Staff to Help Meet PAVE Goals?

Most pre-K and kindergarten classrooms have other adults who help teachers carry out instruction—teacher assistants, early intervention staff, or, if the teacher is lucky, consistent volunteers. In our experience these other adults can be relatively easily trained to carry out important parts of the program, and they can be a tremendous help. In the past we have heard teachers wonder whether supplementary personnel have the education or linguistic skills to serve as good models for students. Yet unless a person has an unusual cognitive limitation (or is a recent speaker of English), surely he or she will have more advanced language skills than the average 4- or 5-year-old child! Most adults can indeed serve as models of oral language learning and can be highly successful in carrying out the small-group activities associated with the program.

Here are some suggestions for supporting others who are helping in the classroom:

1. Provide practice with an adult partner: This can be especially helpful in training assistant teachers and volunteers.

2. Model the basic elements of small-group activities: It would be helpful for support staff and other adults to observe teachers both using CAR Quest prompts in large-group reading sessions and guiding conversations in small-group Building Bridges sessions.

3. Provide adequate time for preparation: In CAR Quest the goal is to spark conversations about the book using the CAR Quest prompts. Adults will need to have read through the book prior to reading it with children.

Each teacher knows best how to use the knowledge, skills, and experience of his or her particular classroom teaching team. Some assistant teachers may be quite experienced, whereas others may have relatively limited classroom experience. The following are areas in which we advise the teacher to assume complete responsibility:

- Selecting or creating units
- Creating a schedule for vocabulary activities
- Communicating the schedule to the assistant or volunteer
- Tracking each child's small-group participation
- Preparing materials for the extension activities
- Posting target items for children to see somewhere in classroom
- Sending home parent communications

## How Do I Involve Families?

It can be incredibly frustrating when parents do not seem to support their children's learning. Teachers' jobs become much easier if they can partner and collaborate with families. But teachers cannot really fault parents for never having learned how to be good collaborators. The good news is that they can teach them how to collaborate, helping them see the importance of vocabulary and oral language skills in their children's learning. By enabling parents to parallel the curriculum at home, teachers can improve children's early literacy skills tremendously (Morrow, Kuhn, & Schwanenflugel, 2006).

## Share the Unit Topic and New Vocabulary Words

Each unit includes a letter that informs parents about the week's topic. These letters include the words that are the primary focus for the week and provide kid-friendly definitions for each word. They also solicit the family's participation in using these words around their children and identifying examples of them around the house if possible.

Most schools have some sort of weekly communication with parents, and these letters can be copied and included with them. In the past we have found that parents grow accustomed to seeing these communiqués, making them an excellent starting point for discussions at parent–teacher conferences. For example, if you keep records regarding which words a child has learned, parents will then become familiar with the program and have concrete evidence of their child's progress in vocabulary learning. You can copy the letters as they are or modify them to better suit your purpose and personal style.

## Share the PAVE Strategies

Many schools have some sort of schoolwide parent group (such as the Parent–Teacher Association), and often schools sponsor a literacy night. These are excellent opportunities to provide the sort of parental training that helps parents support learning at home (Morrow et al., 2006). Teachers can do the following during a parent meeting:

1. Talk with parents about how to read interactively with their child and how to ask different types of questions when they read

2. Demonstrate how parents can support children's language development using Building Bridges principles and discuss why this kind of language is so important

3. Provide parents with activities and suggestions for extending children's learning of the new vocabulary words at home

## Recruit Family Volunteers

As noted earlier, volunteers, including eager parents, can be an excellent source of extra help. A consistent classroom volunteer can carry out some small-group activities with minimal training. Other volunteers who cannot help in the classroom during the day might be recruited to provide some simple materials for extension activities.

## How Can I Assess My Students?

The *PAVEd for Success* program does not include a specific system for assessing children's vocabulary and oral language skills. Teachers have found it helpful to track children's spontaneous use of new vocabulary words; we include such a curriculum-based assessment in Appendix B. Appendix B also includes two general assessments of vocabulary and oral language, one based on language transcripts and the other based on a checklist of various skills.

## A Classroom Example

Mr. Silverstone's kindergarten classroom is looking very crowded. Tonight he has invited families to school for Pajama Reading Night. He introduced PAVE at an earlier kindergarten parent night but now wants to show parents how excited his students are to be talking about books. It is 7 p.m. and parents and children are beginning to arrive. He gathers the children and their parents into a circle. It is cramped, but everyone finds a place. He begins by asking the children if they can tell their parents what this week's topic is. Hands shoot up and children quickly answer: "Stars," "Sunlight," "Getting really, really dark." This week's topic is outer space. Mr. Silverstone summarizes the children's responses and tells parents that the class is learning about daytime and nighttime and what you can see in the sky. He shows families the vocabulary word wall with this week's new vocabulary words and reminds them that these are the words he sent home on Monday. He holds up the picture cards and asks children for the vocabulary labels, as he does each morning when he reviews the new vocabulary. He then reads *Sunshine: A Book About Sunlight* (Sherman, 2004) using the CAR Quest prompts. He has chosen to read the informational text related to the unit to encourage parents to think of different types of books they might read at home.

After reading the book, Mr. Silverstone again asks the children to tell everyone about some of the activities that they have been doing in class this week. The biggest hit seems to be the extension activity, Let's Pretend to Be the Earth, Sun, and Moon, which does not surprise him. Mr. Silverstone briefly talks about how he tries to help the children learn words by using a topic, introducing new vocabulary words, and using these new words in lots of activities throughout the day. He explains to parents how much it will help their children if they can follow up at home.

The last of the evening's activities is parent–child reading. Mr. Silverstone has asked the children to bring in a favorite story from home or to choose a favorite book from the classroom library that they would like to share with their family. He has set up the classroom with as many cozy spots as he can and passes out popcorn, as well. Pajama Reading Night is a lot of work, but his children love it and their families really have a chance to learn what is going on in school.

CHAPTER

# 6

- - -

# Creating Your Own Vocabulary Unit

In the previous chapters we gave examples of what teachers will find in a PAVE vocabulary unit. But what exactly do these units comprise? PAVE units bring together all of the elements we have found useful in developing children's vocabulary: a focus on 10 unfamiliar vocabulary words, picture cards for each new vocabulary word and paired known words to use in introducing them, two trade books related to the topic, CAR Quest prompts for each book, a Building Bridges Start 'em Up! Topic, descriptions of classroom activities to extend vocabulary usage, a classroom vocabulary list, and a family communication letter. All of these elements are organized as a unit related to a specific topic or theme. Using a topical approach makes these experiences more meaningful for children and integrates their experiences with new words.

In response to requests from classroom teachers, we have created 24 vocabulary units that can be used with the *PAVEd for Success* program. Teachers wanted sample units that tied together all of the PAVE strategies. But there is no need to use these units as they are written. Feel free to adapt them to meet your curricular needs, specific content standards that you are expected to cover, or areas that you want to develop more fully as integrated units. Also feel free to develop brand new units of your own using the guidelines we present here (see Table 6.1). Below we describe each of the steps used in creating a unit.

## STEP 1: CHOOSE AN APPROPRIATE TOPIC

As we pondered possible topics for PAVE units, we started with those we thought would be interesting to young children (e.g., Feelings, Animal Babies, Fire Safety), ones that would be typically addressed in pre-K or kindergarten classrooms (e.g., Careers and Community Helpers, Dental Health), as well as those that directly meet science and social studies standards (e.g., Magnets, Recycling and the Environment, Seasons). Although they would have made wonderful learning experiences for children, some of the ideas we considered did not prove useful as topics for a vocabulary unit. An example is families. The English language is just not very rich in

**Table 6.1.**   Steps for creating your own vocabulary unit

Choose an appropriate theme.

Select two related trade books.

Identify 10 unfamiliar vocabulary words.

Create picture cards for the Novel Name–Nameless Category (N3C) strategy.

Create quick definitions.

Write the CAR Quest prompts.

Plan two extension activities.

Develop Building Bridges Start 'em Up! Topics.

Type up the new vocabulary word list for posting in the classroom.

Write the parent communication letter.

vocabulary on this topic—after *cousin, stepmother,* and *parent,* one quickly runs out of words that children do not already know. Thus, not all topic ideas are good vocabulary topics. In selecting a PAVE topic, think *vocabulary first!*

## STEP 2: SELECT BOOKS FOR THE UNIT

The PAVE units include two trade books that relate to the unit topic. As you think of a possible topic, consider the books that might be available on that topic. We found it helpful to gather a selection of books related to the topic, review each book, and then narrow our selection to two by asking the following questions.

### Does the Book Contain Unfamiliar Vocabulary Words Related to the Topic?

The goal of *PAVEd for Success* is to introduce children to new vocabulary words. One of the strengths of traditional children's picture books is their use of rich vocabulary—some old favorites such as *Blueberries for Sal* (McCloskey, 1948) are full of interesting vocabulary words such as *clump* and *partridge.* Unfortunately it seems like the complexity of children's picture books is decreasing (Chamberlain & Leal, 1999); you may have to do some searching to find books with good vocabulary. Some books are unlikely to be good choices. Leveled books associated with typical reading programs tend to contain less challenging vocabulary and generally are not appropriate as a support for vocabulary learning. Some classic favorites that both teachers and their students enjoy (e.g., those by Dr. Seuss) may be excellent for introducing rhyming words but not for learning vocabulary. Within each unit you will introduce 10 new vocabulary words. Ideally the topic-related books you choose will include at least three of those unfamiliar vocabulary words. As you review possible book choices, consider the illustrations as a source of new vocabulary as well as the story text itself. In Bug Helpers one of the unfamiliar vocabulary words is *antenna. Antenna* does not appear in the story text of either book in the unit, but antennae are clearly depicted in the illustrations and might be discussed during the read-aloud or extension activity.

### Am I Including Different Types of Books?

By including books of different types or genres, you not only expose your students to different styles of narratives but also increase your chances of identifying good vocabulary. Informational books often offer more options for vocabulary learning than do storybooks. An alphabet book may seem too easy for kindergarten students but may in fact have more unknown vocabulary words. For example, in our Fire Safety unit we include the informational alphabet book *Firefighters A to Z* (Demarest, 2001) because it contains many words that are likely to be unknown to children. In the Feelings unit we include the fiction book *When Sophie Gets Angry—Really, Really Angry...* (Bang, 1999) as well as the informational book *The Way I Feel* (Cain, 2000). Try to include a broad variety of books as you develop new units. Using both informational books and traditional children's literature will help you meet the new Common Core State Standards for English Language Arts (see Appendix A).

# STEP 3: CHOOSE VOCABULARY WORDS FOR THE UNIT

We have found that 10 new vocabulary words per unit is a manageable number. As you begin reviewing books you may also begin to think of which new vocabulary words to include. Teachers know their students best, and you will recognize which words most of your students do not know. You may find many examples of unknown vocabulary words related to your topic idea; some are better choices than others. Asking yourself the following questions will help you choose words that will be most effective with *PAVEd for Success*.

## Can I Picture the Words Concretely and Distinctly?

For each new vocabulary word, you will need to create picture vocabulary cards similar to those we provide. Thus, the vocabulary words you choose should be ones that can be illustrated concretely and unambiguously. Ideally the pictures should clearly represent the vocabulary word, but not other words, too. Nouns are generally straightforward (*thermometer, excavator, escalator, wharf*); some adjectives will work (*confused, excited*); prepositions generally do not work (*through, under, above*). As you narrow down your choice of unfamiliar words, consider how you could illustrate them.

## Are the Words Useful in More than One Context?

The ideal words are those that children will encounter in more than one situation but that are not so technical that they are unlikely to be used in other contexts. An example might be words related to hospitals: *Stethoscope* would be a better new vocabulary word than *defibrillator*. *Stethoscope* is a word that children are likely to encounter on a typical doctor's visit and one that is often found in children's books. *Defibrillator*, though related to the hospital theme, has a very restricted use.

## Are the Words Connected to the Theme or Topic?

Sometimes books that are related to a topic contain vocabulary words that, although unfamiliar, are not themselves related to the topic. You want children to hear and use their new vocabulary words throughout the many activities included in the unit. If the new words found in a book are not related to the topic—even if the book itself is related to the topic—then it is hard to weave the words into the whole unit. A great example is *Rainbow Fish* (Herbert, 1992). This is an interesting book about friendship and cooperation, but it does not work for building a vocabulary unit on friendship or cooperation. Most of the unfamiliar words in *Rainbow Fish*, such as *scale* or *gills*, are great vocabulary words for a unit related to fish but are not appropriate if the unit theme is friendship. This book, as delightful as it is, lacks a rich vocabulary of friendship-related words.

## Are the Words Challenging?

The level of challenge the vocabulary presents is important. Consider dime words instead of nickel words. *Nickel words* are general, simple words already in children's vocabulary. *Dime words* are more specific, abstract, or categorical. They are unfamiliar words that expand or elaborate on more general and known vocabulary words. (Refer to Table 2.3 in Chapter 2 for some examples of nickel and dime words.)

# STEP 4: DEVELOP INSTRUCTIONAL MATERIALS

Figure 6.1 outlines all of the instructional materials you will need for a unit. Teachers will need to create quick definitions for each new vocabulary word, write CAR Quest prompts for each book, develop Building Bridges Start em' Up Topics, and design or find appropriate vocabulary picture cards.

## Vocabulary Picture Cards

New vocabulary words are introduced and reinforced using picture cards. The picture cards do not have to be artistic masterpieces, but they should clearly represent each vocabulary word, be in color, and have the label or picture for the new vocabulary word typed on them. For the units in Section II, we have selected our own illustrations for the picture cards from clip art and have provided them on the accompanying CD-ROM. Stock photos, clip art, or images collected from other sources will all work. Keep in mind that you will need some pictures of known words that can be used in the N3C introduction of vocabulary too, but you can feel free to use ours.

## Quick Definitions

Quick definitions are used as part of the N3C vocabulary introduction technique and are used to reinforce the new vocabulary words each day. The nontechnical, kid-friendly definition should fit the way the vocabulary word is used in the topic and related books. The quick definitions found in the Dental Health unit illustrate this point (see Table 6.2). All of these words actually have alternative definitions: *Braces* can be used to support a building or a broken leg, a *cavity* can be a hidden hole, a *drill* can be used by a carpenter, and *gum* can be chewed by children. These meanings are not included in the quick definitions because they do not reflect the usage of the words in the related books or themes. Quick definitions should be helpful for clarifying new vocabulary as you read the books and for talking about the new vocabulary during the extension activities.

## CAR Quest Prompts

For each book included in the unit, you will need six CAR Quest prompts. Create two prompts from each of the following categories (see Table 3.2 for examples of each type of prompt):

- *Competence* prompts ask students to identify information that is directly in front of them, either in the text or the picture.
- *Abstract* prompts ask students to go beyond the immediate information in the text.
- *Relate* prompts ask students to make personal connections with the storybook.

## Building Bridges Start 'em Up! Topics

Although Building Bridges conversations do not have to be about the unit topics, many teachers find it helpful to use the unit topic as a starting point for initiating small-group conversations.

# PAVE Weekly Lesson Plan
# Contents for Teacher-Created Units

- - - - - - - - - - - - - - - - - - - - - - - - - - - - - - - - - - - - - - - -

**Dates:** _____

**Unit topic:** _____

✓ Identify 10 vocabulary words related to topic.

1. _____
2. _____
3. _____
4. _____
5. _____
6. _____
7. _____
8. _____
9. _____
10. _____

✓ Select two books related to topic.

1. _____
2. _____
3. _____ (optional)

✓ Create a quick definition for each vocabulary word.

| No. | Vocabulary word | Quick definition |
|-----|-----------------|------------------|
|     |                 |                  |
|     |                 |                  |
|     |                 |                  |
|     |                 |                  |
|     |                 |                  |
|     |                 |                  |
|     |                 |                  |
|     |                 |                  |
|     |                 |                  |
|     |                 |                  |

**Figure 6.1.** *PAVEd for Success* Weekly Lesson Plan Contents for Teacher-Created Units form.

*(continued)*

## PAVE Weekly Lesson Plan Contents for Teacher-Created Units (continued)

✓ Select pictures of each vocabulary word and known words to be used with the Novel Name–Nameless Category (N3C) vocabulary introduction strategy.

| No. | Vocabulary word | Known word 1 | Known word 2 |
|-----|-----------------|--------------|--------------|
|     |                 |              |              |
|     |                 |              |              |
|     |                 |              |              |
|     |                 |              |              |
|     |                 |              |              |
|     |                 |              |              |
|     |                 |              |              |
|     |                 |              |              |
|     |                 |              |              |
|     |                 |              |              |
|     |                 |              |              |

✓ Develop six questions for each book for read-aloud based on CAR Quest method.

| Book | Type | Question |
|------|------|----------|
| Book 1: | Competence question 1 | |
|         | Competence question 2 | |
|         | Abstract question 1 | |
|         | Abstract question 2 | |
|         | Relate question 1 | |
|         | Relate question 2 | |
| Book 2: | Competence question 1 | |
|         | Competence question 2 | |
|         | Abstract question 1 | |
|         | Abstract question 2 | |
|         | Relate question 1 | |
|         | Relate question 2 | |

✓ Develop Building Bridges Start 'em Up! Topic: _____

(continued)

# PAVE Weekly Lesson Plan Contents for Teacher-Created Units (continued)

✓ Organize two extension activities that allow children to extend and utilize their emerging knowledge of the vocabulary words.

| Extension activity | Description | Materials needed |
|---|---|---|
| Activity 1: | | |
| Activity 2: | | |

✓ Create a family letter or other communication that contains the target words for the week.

✓ Create a posting for the classroom vocabulary wall.

**Table 6.2.**  Examples of quick definitions

| Word | Definition |
|------|------------|
| *braces* | wires or other materials that dentists use to straighten your teeth |
| *cavity* | a hole in your tooth that the dentist fixes |
| *drill* | what the dentist uses to fix a cavity |
| *gum* | the pink stuff in your mouth that holds your teeth |

All of the units in Section II include Building Bridges Start 'em Up! Topics that can help get the conversation going. You can use these starters as part of a small-group extension activity or at the conclusion of a small-group book-reading session. A note of caution: Keep the topics open ended to encourage conversation and to avoid merely rehearsing taught material. Keep in mind that the purpose is conversation and not content recall. For example, in the Feelings unit, the Building Bridges Start 'em Up! Topic is "What feelings did you have this morning before you came to school?" There is no correct answer to this question; it is open ended and invites the children to engage in conversations about topics that interest them. Let the conversation drift the way that conversations with adults do.

## STEP 5: PLAN EXTENSION ACTIVITIES

Each PAVE unit includes at least two extension activities. The goal of these activities is to encourage children's use of unfamiliar vocabulary across different settings. The activities themselves do not have to be complicated. By talking with one another and perhaps with an adult as they do these activities, children will gain practice in using the words in their own speech. It does not matter when the activities are scheduled within the school day or where they are carried out. Possibilities include activities planned for centers, free play, small-group work time, or a science or social studies block.

Many of the activities we include in the PAVE units extend children's conceptual understanding of the unit topic. In the Feelings unit one of the extension activities involves giving children a mirror and letting them make emotion faces with a partner, perhaps at their desks, in the dramatic play area, or as part of a small-group activity. Another activity included in the Feelings unit is the making of an emotion collage. This might be done as part of a creation station or table-sorting activity during centers, a craft activity during art, or a small-group activity during social studies. These activities are not complicated and do not require a lot of materials. What is important is that they give children practice in hearing and speaking their new vocabulary words in ways that a book on tape or an independent worksheet cannot.

Extension activities can also include general classroom vocabulary games that are adapted to the unit theme. Some examples are

- *Vocabulary bingo.* Bingo sets can be made using the picture cards and the game played in small groups or as a whole-class activity.

- *Vocabulary center.* A special vocabulary center can be set up for use during free play or independent work time. This center might have a three-ring binder containing the picture cards and labels. Children can create their own illustrations to add to the binder.

- *Vocabulary show-and-tell table.* Ask students to bring an object from home or a drawing that they have done depicting one of the unfamiliar vocabulary words. During the morning meeting students can share their new vocabulary word with the class. These pictures or objects can later be displayed on a small table.

- *Book prop baskets or flannel board stories.* Many teachers find it helpful to develop prop baskets or flannel boards to go along with the topic-related books. Prop baskets include objects that depict the vocabulary words that occur in the book. These boxes are placed on a shelf or table with the book. Flannel board stories traditionally include the major characters and features found in a storybook and are used as the teacher reads the book aloud. You can modify this a bit to emphasize the unfamiliar vocabulary and have students "read" these to one another during small-group or center time.

- *Vocabulary concentration.* You can reformat your picture cards in smaller formats to use in a game of concentration. Children can play vocabulary concentration in pairs or by themselves.

# STEP 6: COMMUNICATE TO OTHERS THE VOCABULARY BEING FOCUSED ON IN THE CLASSROOM

Children will be more successful in learning new vocabulary when they have as many opportunities as possible to hear and use new vocabulary words. It is important that all of the adults in the classroom—teachers, assistant teachers, and volunteers—are familiar with the new vocabulary words.  Letting families know what the unit topic and the new vocabulary are will provide even more opportunities for children to learn new vocabulary words.

## Classroom Posting

For each unit in Section II we have included a list of the new vocabulary words to be posted in the classroom. This list is really for the adults in the classroom; they may need a reminder to focus on the new vocabulary. Of course labels, pictures, or a combination of labels and pictures can also be used to display the new vocabulary. These are also available on the accompanying CD-ROM.

## Family Letters

Sharing the unit topic and new vocabulary words with families will help them support learning at home. Feel free to use the sample letter we have included with each unit and on the accompanying CD-ROM as a template for communicating with families.

Over the years many of the teachers we have worked with have shared with us units that they have developed. We have been amazed but not surprised by how wonderful these units are. Give it a try! Figure 6.1 contains a lesson plan rubric that you can use to create your own unit. The units you develop will be the ones you and your students enjoy the most.

# Supporting the Needs of Diverse Learners

**D**iversity is a central feature of early childhood programs. Children in today's classrooms come from various socioeconomic backgrounds, have different ethnic and cultural heritages, are often likely to be English language learners (ELLs), and not infrequently have disabilities. There is often diversity in terms of age as well. Educators may teach in multiage classrooms that enroll children with a broad range of developmental competencies. Diversity and difference are the norm rather than the exception in early childhood settings (Genishi & Dyson, 2009). We designed *PAVEd for Success* to be appropriate for working with diverse learners. Teachers have effectively used PAVE in classrooms serving ethnically and culturally diverse populations of students, including ELLs as well as children with special needs.

One may wonder what changes or accommodations would be most appropriate for implementing PAVE in such a classroom. In this chapter we focus specifically on ELLs and children with special needs. Nonetheless, the accommodations we describe as well as the framework we present are applicable to a variety of diverse learners.

## ENGLISH LANGUAGE LEARNERS

Almost 25% of all schoolchildren in the United States come from homes in which a language other than English is spoken (National Center for Education Statistics [NCES], 2010). The proportion of ELLs enrolled in U.S. schools has steadily increased since the late 1990s and will continue to increase in the future. Unfortunately, schools do not seem able to meet the educational needs of many of these children. Children of immigrants, those who are learning to speak English, and those who are growing up in poverty face a host of challenges and are more likely to be at risk for academic difficulties (Restrepo & Dubasik, 2008). Luckily, those enrolled in high-quality early childhood settings with appropriate language supports can overcome these risks.

In thinking about children who speak languages other than English, it is helpful to distinguish between those who have been learning two or more languages since birth and those who arrive in early childhood programs just beginning to learn English. Children who learn two languages at the same time develop skills in both languages similar to monolingual or English-only children. Those who are learning a second language sequentially (e.g., those who perhaps have been speaking Spanish at home and are now enrolled in an English-speaking pre-K or kindergarten program) tend to go through the following predictable stages in their acquisition of the new language (Restrepo & Dubasik, 2008; Tabors, 2008):

- *Stage 1:* Initially, some children may try to communicate in the new setting using their home language. They may seem either unaware or confused that others do not easily understand them. As they realize that their teachers and peers do not understand them, they may withdraw from verbal interactions.

- *Stage 2:* Withdrawal leads to a silent period. Children no longer rely on their home language, though they may attempt to communicate nonverbally with gestures.

- *Stage 3:* Gradually, as children begin to use their new language, they are faced with the challenge of communicating with limited vocabulary and understanding how their new language works. They may use one or two words to stand for more complex ideas, or, if they use complete sentences or phrases, they may not completely understand what they are saying. They are beginning to communicate and they may be somewhat successful during predictable classroom routines, but they are still limited in terms of the ideas they can express and understand in the new language.

- *Stage 4:* The transition to productive language use is marked by the use of longer sentences, increased vocabulary, and comprehension. Children may continue to make some grammatical errors in their speech, their vocabulary in the new language may still be somewhat restricted, and they may code-switch or mix the home language with English (e.g., "My mama, she bought *leche* at the grocery").

Most children learning a new language will go through these stages. Yet this does not mean that all ELLs are the same. Some ELLs live in poverty, some have parents who are fluent and highly educated in both languages, some may have just moved to the United States, some may have a disability—there are differences beyond language that influence children's English language acquisition.

## CHILDREN WITH SPECIAL NEEDS

Approximately 13% of all children enrolled in public school receive services through the Individuals with Disabilities Education Act of 1990 (PL 101-476). While children may receive services for a variety of disabilities, the most common services for young children revolve around communication disorders. The purpose of most of these special education services is to provide intervention for speech and language problems that are associated with language impairments directly or a related diagnosis such as autism spectrum disorder. Unlike ELLs, the overall number of children with disabilities has remained stable since the 1990s. However, there are more children with special needs in general education settings. This is especially true of children who have speech or language impairments. More than 80% of children with language-related disorders now spend most of their day in general education settings (NCES, 2010).

Though children with disabilities may be included in general education classrooms, the simple fact of being present does not mean that these children are receiving the same benefits from classroom literacy activities as their peers who are typically developing. This is especially true for children with significant language or intellectual disabilities as well as for those with more moderate language impairments (Browder et al., 2009). Children with special needs may participate as often as their peers in literacy activities, and they may be read to just as frequently. But how they experience an activity such as shared reading may be quite different from how their classmates who are typically developing do (Crowe, Norris, & Hoffman, 2004; Justice & Kaderavek, 2002). Why? Children with language impairments often produce minimal or negative verbal responses during shared book readings, and they may remain quiet and passive. In an effort to structure the interaction, their parents and teachers may then respond by being more directive and controlling, further limiting the children's interaction and engagement (Crowe et al., 2004). It is not surprising, then, that many children with disabilities begin to find shared book reading to be a negative experience and soon have little motivation to engage in literacy-related activities (Justice & Kaderavek, 2002). All children, regardless of their abilities, need access to high-quality early literacy instruction. Yet the children who may benefit the most from PAVE may be those most difficult to engage.

## UNIVERSAL DESIGN FOR LEARNING

How can teachers meet the needs of diverse learners in the classroom? How can they get all children off to the right start? This complex challenge can be overwhelming—where to begin? A framework we have found useful in thinking about adapting curriculum is Universal Design for Learning (UDL). In this section we present an overview of the principles underlying UDL and discuss how they can be used to adapt PAVE to fit the needs of diverse students. Although we present examples specifically for children with language impairments and ELLs, the UDL framework can be useful more generally for making any curriculum accessible for a wide range of diverse learners.

UDL was developed out of the work done through the Center for Applied Special Technology (CAST) on assistive technology. Its primary purpose is to expand learning opportunities for all students regardless of their disability status. (For more information see the web site of the National Center on Universal Design for Learning at http://www.udlcenter.org/.) When designing a curriculum, a program, or even an individual lesson plan within the principles of UDL, one should allow for multiple means of representation of, action and expression with, and engagement with the content (National Center on Universal Design for Learning, 2010). The overall design of PAVE already reflects these guiding principles:

1. *Multiple means of representation* refers to how children are provided with different options for acquiring information and knowledge. When they use this principle, PAVE teachers are adjusting how they present information, not the content of the information they present. This can be seen in New VEhicles in terms of how teachers introduce vocabulary: visually through introducing new words pictorially using the N3C strategy, and orally through quick definitions and interactive storybook reading. The content and unfamiliar vocabulary words are the same; the ways in which teachers present the content vary and so are more accessible to children with different learning needs.

2. *Multiple means of action and expression* refers to how children can interact with the content and show what they know. Think about the different levels of CAR Quest prompts, reading

in both small-group and whole-class settings, and the reinforcement of new vocabulary through extension activities. Children can show what they know about the book they are listening to by relating it to their own lives (Relate prompts), by directly using the story text or illustration (Competence prompts), and by making predictions and solving problems about the narrative (Abstract prompts). They can demonstrate their understanding of the new vocabulary through their use of language in extension activities. They can participate in both small- and large-group settings.

3. *Multiple means of engagement* suggests that teachers look at the various ways in which they can tap into children's interests, offer appropriate challenges, and increase motivation. Teachers often struggle with maintaining children's attention to the task at hand; if children do not attend and are not engaged, they do not learn. Building on student interest is key to engaging students. CAR Quest includes Relate prompts that ask children to relate the book directly to their own lives. Similarly, in Building Bridges teachers follow the children's conversational lead. These strategies encourage children to relate content to their own individual interests. In addition, both Building Bridges and CAR Quest offer children different levels of challenge.

## ACCOMMODATIONS AND *PAVEd FOR SUCCESS*

The principles of UDL, which are evident throughout PAVE, can be extended and used as a framework to develop additional accommodations for ELLs, children with disabilities, and other learners. We have organized our discussion of accommodations around the individual PAVE strategies.

### Building Bridges

The goal of Building Bridges is to engage children in conversations. The Building Bridges Start 'em Up! Topics are conversation openers teachers can use during small-group extension activities or shared book-reading sessions. For many children conversations will flow naturally in these settings; typically, young children are interested in talking about new topics. For children who are just beginning to learn English or who have less advanced oral language skills, talking about *new* topics and using *new* vocabulary during *new* activities may be too much of a challenge. There is simply too much to think about. Children may be more comfortable and engaged when conversations concern typical routines or typical play activities using more familiar vocabulary. Scheduling Building Bridges as part of mealtime, during classroom transitions, or during free-play activities may be more effective. Children are likely to be more successful if they are grouped with other children with similar language skills.

### CAR Quest

For bilingual children, supporting language development in both the home language and English is preferable. Yet this is much easier said than done in most early childhood classrooms: Few teachers are fluent in all of the languages that may be spoken by the children in their classrooms. What can a teacher do when he or she does not speak or read a child's home languages? Many of the children's books we have included in the units in Section II are available in Spanish (see Appendix B). If teachers have a support person in their classroom or if they themselves speak Spanish, these books can be read as part of the small-group book-reading sessions. Children can also be provided with audio versions of the books. Teachers may already have a listening center in their classroom in which children can listen to books independently. As support for book discussions we also suggest pairing children who share a home language and having them listen and talk quietly about the book. Teachers can also engage parents who speak Spanish by asking them to record themselves reading books in Spanish.

Teachers can also make changes in how they read books. Use of a flannel board is a traditional approach used to make storytelling more creative and to offer more visual support during reading. Providing the flannel board characters to children during small-group reading sessions or for independent use in a library corner will offer them more interactive ways to engage with the content. Technology also offers many opportunities for interaction. More and more children's titles are now becoming available as digital books. Digital books may be copies of the original or may also include simple animations or film clips as explanations for concepts. Teachers can use an LCD projector to display the book during large-group reading sessions. Reading a book in this way solves the "I can't see the pictures!" problem, is likely to be engaging for students, and is certainly more appropriate for children with postural or visual impairments. Finally, finding more creative ways of reading books may be needed to capture the attention of children with language impairments who may not have much interest in book reading.

CAR Quest discussions are another area in which to develop accommodations. Here teachers want to think about the different ways in which less verbal children or those with limited English proficiency can respond to the CAR Quest prompts. Asking questions that reduce the language demands of the child is most effective. Prompting children to point or use gestures in answer to a question is a way to enable them to join in the conversation even if their verbal responses are limited. For example, in a small-group reading session teachers could offer children flannel board characters and phrase their CAR Quest prompts so that the children can answer by holding up or pointing to the appropriate character. Offering a few pages copied from the storybook itself or providing individual picture cards is a good way to reduce the language demands of the task but still involve children with the story; they can point or hold up a picture as a response. Reading in smaller groups or in more cozy areas (e.g., on pillows in a library corner rather than at a small table) may further encourage reluctant readers and make it easier for teachers to attend to nonverbal responses.

## New VEhicles

Within New VEhicles, unfamiliar vocabulary words are introduced and reinforced through N3C, quick definitions, repeated readings of books with embedded vocabulary, and extension activities. As teachers use New VEhicles they will give children lots of opportunities to hear and use the new words they are learning. For children with disabilities or those who are learning English as a second language, even more opportunities would be better! In the classroom example in Chapter 4, Ms. Silva conducted the extension activities included in the unit *and* carried the unit topic of fire safety across multiple areas of her classroom. Children in her classroom had multiple ways to engage with the material. Her approach builds on children's spontaneous—though perhaps adult-facilitated—use of new vocabulary words. In Chapter 4 we also suggest ways for teachers to incorporate activities that more intentionally and directly target vocabulary learning through Vocabulary Bingo, Treasure Hunts, Concentration, Show and Tell, and Vocabulary Centers.

The primary premise of UDL is that curriculum should be accessible to all children and that increasing accessibility will benefit all learners. This framework guided much of our design for PAVE, and we think it will be useful for teachers to use when adapting the PAVE strategies to their individual learners.

## A Classroom Example:
## Prekindergarten (Inclusive Special Education)

Ms. Monroe teaches in an inclusive pre-K classroom serving fifteen 3- and 4-year-olds who are typically and atypically developing. In addition to Ms. Monroe, the teaching staff includes two assistant teachers and various professionals who come into the classroom throughout the day to provide specialized intensive services. Children attend for half-day sessions and leave after lunch. Ms. Monroe uses a play-based curriculum with free-play exploration of centers occurring throughout most of the day. Children are together in a whole group twice a day: early in the morning for meet and greet and later after recess for whole-group reading. There are no scheduled small-group activities.

When the children arrive on Wednesday, Ms. Monroe gathers them on the rug for morning circle. During this time she encourages peer interaction and use of social skills. She is also using this time to reinforce the new vocabulary words about feelings for the Feelings unit they are doing. She places the picture vocabulary cards on the rug and leads the children in singing *Where Oh Where Is My Friend…?* As she points to Jess the children sing his name and Jess reaches for the picture card illustrating *angry,* saying, "I am very, very angry that my little brother knocked over my LEGOs." Ms. Monroe smiles; Jess is always a big talker, and certainly he has been listening carefully to this week's book, *When Sophie Gets Angry—Really, Really Angry….* The next child in the circle is Marissa, a 3-year-old with developmental delays. As Ms. Monroe points to Marissa, the children sing her name, and Marissa glances up and briefly looks at the *excited* picture card. Ms. Monroe has been watching carefully for a nonverbal response and elaborates on Marissa's response by saying, "It looks like Marissa might be excited today. I wonder if she thinks something fun is going to happen." There is a long pause and then another child jumps in with, "Maybe her mama is getting her ice *crema.*" Ms. Monroe nods and says, "Maybe getting her ice cream could make someone excited. Maybe Marissa will tell us more about it later." The children and Ms. Monroe continue singing, with each child having a turn; some children elaborate on the feeling words themselves. For others like Marissa, Ms. Monroe expands their gestures or simple responses with the quick definition for the vocabulary word. At the end of the song Ms. Monroe points to the picture cards not chosen by any of the children, asking for the appropriate labels and providing a quick definition.

Morning circle has gone on long enough, so Ms. Monroe shows the children the cover of *When Sophie Gets Angry—Really, Really Angry…* and tells them that this is the new book they will be reading later after outside time. She concludes circle by asking the children to choose which center they want to begin with. She reminds them that they can do emotion collages in the art area with Ms. Kelly, use the mirrors in the dramatic play area, play concentration in the table games area, or join her in the book nook for a preview reading of *When Sophie Gets Angry—Really, Really Angry….* During free play Ms. Monroe schedules herself and the assistant teachers into different centers rather than the children into small groups. In each center she has posted the week's vocabulary words and a list of children's names so that she can check to make sure each child has engaged in small-group book reading or an extension activity related to the unit topic. After free play and outside time, the children gather on the rug for storytime. Ms. Monroe introduces *When Sophie Gets Angry—Really, Really Angry…* with a book walk and then reads the story with CAR Quest prompts. This is the first time most of the children will hear the story. Some heard the story earlier during free play—Ms. Monroe tries to preview a new book with a couple of the children who have been less interested in the group storytimes.

Children in her classroom often need assistance or, in some cases, receive direct services during mealtimes. Meal and snack times are when Ms. Monroe has scheduled Building Bridges. This approach seems to work best for her children. Fortunately, she was able to schedule a session on PAVE during the afternoon team planning time. All of the adults in her classroom, including the special education support staff and her assistants, have learned how to conduct Building Bridges conversations.

## A Classroom Example: Kindergarten

Mr. Li teaches kindergarten in a public school located in a moderate-sized urban area. Approximately 60% of his 33 students are ELLs, and most come from Spanish-speaking homes. Support for students learning English is provided as a pull-out program, and several of his students leave the classroom during various parts of the day. He and another kindergarten teacher share an assistant teacher. This week his class is doing the unit Magnets. Mr. Li chose this topic because it relates to one of the state standards he needs to cover and is included in the science kit curriculum used in his school.

He schedules the PAVE extension activities during the afternoon science block. In the morning during the literacy block he has an assistant teacher; this is when he schedules the small-group book-reading sessions. During the literacy block Mr. Li provides small-group instruction using the district-approved literacy curriculum. The assistant teacher works with another small group carrying out CAR Quest followed by Building Bridges conversations. There are three independent areas: a vocabulary center, a listening center, and phonics games. One of this week's topic books, *Magnets: Pulling Together, Pushing Apart* (Rosinsky, 2003), is available in Spanish. One of Mr. Li's parents has agreed to read some of the books in Spanish and make audio recordings for him. He uses these Spanish-language tapes in the listening center and allows two or three children to listen and talk quietly about the book as they read along.

The assistant teacher leads most of the Building Bridges conversations. However, to support the ELLs in his classroom Mr. Li tries to schedule two Building Bridges sessions a week during snack time. He mixes the groups up a bit but specifically targets all of his ELL students. Mr. Li also tries to support language during the extension activities in the afternoon science block. Fortunately, some of his science curriculum materials include Spanish-language translations and concept cards; he provides these as well as the PAVE picture cards to his students.

# Vocabulary Units

## INDIVIDUAL UNIT ALIGNMENT WITH SCIENCE AND SOCIAL STUDIES TOPICS

This section presents 24 PAVE vocabulary units. The vocabulary units are ordered by primary content area. Science and social studies content often includes a related focus. A good example is the Landforms unit. Geography is typically studied within social studies; however, the books and extension activities included in this unit also reference the formation of landforms, which relates to concepts typically taught in earth and space science. Many of the vocabulary units include activities related to both science and social studies; the primary content is designated with a • and the secondary content with a ✓.

| Content area | Unit title | Science | Social studies |
|---|---|:---:|:---:|
| **Science** | | | |
| | Animal Babies (p. 59) | • | |
| | Bug Helpers (p. 64) | • | |
| | Dental Health (p. 69) | • | ✓ |
| | Feelings (p.74) | • | |
| | Gardening (p. 79) | • | |
| | Living in the Earth: Worms and Pill Bugs (p. 84) | • | |
| | Magnets (p. 89) | • | |
| | Outer Space (p. 94) | • | ✓ |
| | Recycling and the Environment (p. 99) | • | ✓ |
| | Solids, Liquids, and Gases (p. 104) | • | |
| | Trains and Bridges (p. 109) | • | ✓ |
| | Transportation (p. 114) | • | ✓ |
| **Social Studies** | | | |
| | Hooray for School! (p. 119) | | • |
| | Careers and Community Helpers (p. 124) | | • |
| | Fire Safety (p. 129) | | • |
| | Food Preparation (p. 135) | ✓ | • |
| | Landforms (p. 140) | ✓ | • |
| | Maps and Globes (p. 145) | ✓ | • |
| | Medieval Times (p. 150) | | • |
| | Music (p. 155) | | • |

*(continued)*

*(continued)*

| Content area | Unit title | Science | Social studies |
|---|---|:---:|:---:|
| | Primary Land Uses: Farming and Fishing (p. 160) | ✓ | • |
| | Seasons (p. 165) | ✓ | • |
| | Weather (p. 170) | ✓ | • |
| | Winter (p. 175) | ✓ | • |

# Animal Babies

---

## Vocabulary

| | |
|---|---|
| calf | foal |
| chick | fur |
| cub | hatch |
| fawn | parents |
| feathers | whiskers |

## New VEhicles—
## N3C Vocabulary Introduction

### Initial Presentation

Find pictures for all vocabulary words listed below as well as the two known words paired with each vocabulary word. The known words should be in children's vocabularies. If not, substitute another from the set of pictures that your students are likely to know. In the large-group setting show all three pictures (the vocabulary word and the two known words) randomly to the children and ask them, "Which one is _____?" (insert vocabulary word). The children should be able to infer that the vocabulary word refers to the unknown picture among the three. If you wish, the quick definitions can be introduced then as well. All pictures are included on the accompanying CD-ROM.

| Vocabulary words | Known words |
|---|---|
| calf | chicken, dog |
| chick | butterfly, flower |
| cub | bird, brush |
| fawn | piano, fish |
| feathers | shoe, dress |
| foal | clown, dog |
| fur | coat, fish |
| hatch | cat, jump |
| parents | teacher, doctor |
| whiskers | spoon, ear |

### Subsequent Presentation

After the initial presentation the pictures of the known words can be put away. The rest of the week, display only the pictures of the vocabulary words and say to children, "Show me _____" (insert vocabulary word) or "What's the word for this?" (point at picture).

## Quick Definitions

**calf** a baby cow, elephant, whale, or seal

**chick** a baby chicken or bird

**cub** a baby animal that eats meat, like a lion, tiger, bear, or wolf

**fawn** a baby deer

**feathers** what's on the outside of birds

**foal** a baby horse, mule, or zebra

**fur** the hairy coat covering many animals (mammals, in particular)

**hatch** to break out of an egg

**parents** people who take care of children

**whiskers** the long, stiff hairs growing around an animal's mouth

## CAR Quest

The following are questions that you can ask students about the story you are reading. We suggest reviewing the text beforehand and using sticky notes to mark appropriate places to pause for discussion. The questions are labeled according to the types described in Chapter 3.

### Books

Guarino, D. (1989). *Is your mama a llama?* New York: Scholastic Press.

Simon, S. (2002). *Baby animals.* San Francisco: Chronicle Books.

Page location describes the picture (illustration or photo) that relates to the individual CAR Quest question. Unknown vocabulary words are *italicized*.

### *Is Your Mama a Llama?*

**Page location:** Mama swan with baby on back

 **Competence:** What do the baby's *feathers* look like? What color are the mama's *feathers*?

**Page location:** Mama cow with *calf*

 **Competence:** What does the *calf* look like?

**Page location:** Mama seal with baby

 **Abstract:** These here are the seal's *whiskers*. See them? What other animals have *whiskers*?

**Page location:** Lloyd (brown llama) talking to Llyn (white llama)

 **Abstract:** How do you think a llama's *fur* feels?

 **Relate:** Would you want to have *fur*?

**Page location:** Baby llamas running to their mothers

 **Relate:** These baby animals all talk about their mamas, telling what they look like and what they do. How would you describe your *parents*?

### *Baby Animals*

**Page location:** Mother horse with *foal*

 **Abstract:** Where do you think the *foal* is going?

**Page location:** Lion *cub*

  **Relate:** Have you ever seen a *cub* before—maybe at the zoo?

  **Relate:** Would you want to take care of a newborn *cub*?

**Page location:** Two baby *chicks*

  **Competence:** Where is the baby *chick*? Can anyone point to the baby *chick*?

**Page location:** Mother cow with *calf*

  **Competence:** Is the *calf* bigger or smaller than the mama cow?

  **Abstract:** It says the *calf* drinks milk from its mother. Can you think of any other animals that drink milk when they are babies?

# Building Bridges— Start 'em Up! Topic

We've been talking about animal families. Tell me about your family.

# New VEhicles— Extension Activities

## Activity 1: Animal Matching Concentration Game

**Materials:** Pictures of *foal*, horse, *fawn*, deer, *chick*, chicken, *cub*, polar bear, *calf*, cow, *whiskers*, cat, *fur*, dog, owl, *feather*

**Description:** Children will arrange the pictures face down and try to match the adult animal with its baby and the animal attribute with the animal. Special attention should be placed on using the vocabulary (e.g., "Does the bird have *feathers*?" "Where do you think the newborn *cub's parents* are?").

## Activity 2: Guess the Animal

**Materials:** Pictures of baby animals and their *parents* (the same pictures from Activity 1 could be used)

**Description:** Students will receive a picture and describe that baby animal to the other children. They will describe the covering of the animal (e.g., *feathers*, *fur*, *whiskers*), what the baby animal is called (e.g., *cub*, *chick*, *calf*, *foal*, *fawn*), what color the animal is, and where it lives. Other children in the class will try to guess what parent animal the student is describing.

# Communication

We provide two types of communication: a classroom posting for students and visitors and a parent letter to be sent home. These can be found on the next two pages and on the accompanying CD-ROM.

# Animal Babies Vocabulary Words

calf

chick

cub

fawn

feathers

foal

fur

hatch

parents

whiskers

*PAVEd for Success: Building Vocabulary and Language Development in Young Learners,* by Claire E. Hamilton & Paula J. Schwanenflugel.

Dear Parents:

This week we will be focusing on vocabulary words for Animal Babies. We will be reading stories and carrying out activities to help your child learn the meanings of these words. By pointing out examples of these words at home and in the community, you can help your child expand his or her vocabulary. This week's words (with simple definitions that children can understand) are as follows:

| | |
|---|---|
| calf | a baby cow, elephant, whale, or seal |
| chick | a baby chicken or bird |
| cub | a baby animal that eats meat, like a lion, tiger, bear, or wolf |
| fawn | a baby deer |
| feathers | what's on the outside of birds |
| foal | a baby horse, mule, or zebra |
| fur | the hairy coat covering many animals (mammals, in particular) |
| hatch | to break out of an egg |
| parents | people who take care of children |
| whiskers | the long, stiff hairs growing around an animal's mouth |

Please post this where you and your child can see it. Thanks!

Sincerely,

Your child's teacher

UNIT

**2**
# Bug Helpers

## Vocabulary

| | |
|---|---|
| aphid | praying mantis |
| beetle | tarantula |
| claws | waist |
| dragonfly | wasp |
| ladybug | web |

## New VEhicles—
## N3C Vocabulary Introduction

### Initial Presentation

Find pictures for all vocabulary words listed below as well as the two known words paired with each vocabulary word. The known words should be in children's vocabularies. If not, substitute another from the set of pictures that your students are likely to know. In the large-group setting show all three pictures (the vocabulary word and the two known words) randomly to the children and ask them, "Which one is _____?" (insert vocabulary word). The children should be able to infer that the vocabulary word refers to the unknown picture among the three. If you wish, the quick definitions can be introduced then as well. All pictures are included in the accompanying CD-ROM.

| Vocabulary words | Known words |
|---|---|
| aphid | bird, elephant |
| beetle | chicken, spider |
| claws | arm, carrot |
| dragonfly | spider, flag |
| ladybug | plane, dog |
| praying mantis | elephant, frog |
| tarantula | cow, egg |
| waist | snowman, pants |
| wasp | cow, egg |
| web | bag, table |

### Subsequent Presentation

After the initial presentation the pictures of the known words can be put away. The rest of the week, display only the pictures of the vocabulary words and say to children, "Show me _____" (insert vocabulary word) or "What's the word for this?" (point at picture).

## Quick Definitions

**aphid**   a small green bug that lives on plants

**beetle**   a bug that eats dead things like fallen trees

**claws**   a sharp curved nail at the end of a leg

**dragonfly**   a bug with big wings that eats mosquitoes

**ladybug**   a small bug that's usually orange-red with black spots

**praying mantis**   a big green bug that catches bugs with its hands

**tarantula**   a large hairy spider

**waist**   the middle part of your body

**wasp**   a flying bug that stings and is usually brown

**web**   the thing that spiders make to trap food

## CAR Quest

The following are questions that you can ask students about the story you are reading. We suggest reviewing the text beforehand and using sticky notes to mark appropriate places to pause for discussion. The questions are labeled according to the types described in Chapter 3.

### Books

Allen, J., & Humphries, T. (2000). *Are you a spider?* London: Kingfisher.

Allen, J., & Humphries, T. (2003). *Are you a ladybug?* London: Kingfisher.

Page location describes the picture (illustration or photo) that relates to the individual CAR Quest question. Unknown vocabulary words are *italicized*.

### *Are You a Spider?*

**Page location:** Close-up picture of a spider's body (*waist*, *claws*, spinnerets, legs)

   **Competence:** Where is the *waist* on the spider?

**Page location:** A spider begins to spin a *web*.

   **Abstract:** Why is the spider spinning the *web*?

   **Relate:** Where have you seen a spider hanging from a *web*?

**Page location:** Close-up picture of a *wasp*

   **Competence:** What colors do you see on the *wasp*?

   **Abstract:** Why would you want to be careful around *wasps*?

   **Relate:** Has anyone seen a *wasp* before? Has anyone been stung by a *wasp*?

### *Are You a Ladybug?*

**Page location:** First picture, two *ladybugs* on yellow flowers

   **Competence:** Can you find the *ladybugs*?

   **Relate:** Has anyone here seen a *ladybug* before?

   **Abstract:** Do you think all *ladybugs* are girls? Why do you think they call it a *ladybug*?

**Page location:** Newly hatched *ladybug* eating its eggshell on a leaf with three aphids

   **Abstract:** Why would a *ladybug* want to eat the eggshell?

**Page location:** Newly hatched *ladybug* chasing three *aphids*

> **Relate:** Would you want to eat an *aphid*?

> **Competence:** Can you see the *aphids* in the picture? How many legs do they have?

# Building Bridges— Start 'em Up! Topic

Do you like bugs? Why?

# New VEhicles— Extension Activities

### Activity 1: Bug Food Webs

**Materials:** Paper; pencil; pictures of *ladybug, praying mantis, dragonfly, beetle,* twig, *tarantula, aphid*

**Description:** The teacher will explain how food webs show that different organisms are dependent on one another because of what they eat. Children will draw pictures of the various bugs eating what they eat (e.g., *ladybugs* and *praying mantises* eat *aphids* and *beetles, dragonflies* eat mosquitoes, *beetles* eat old twigs, *tarantulas* eat all other insects).

### Activity 2: Create a Bug Story

**Materials:** Paper, pencil, or other writing instruments

**Description:** Have each child select a bug helper he or she would like to draw. They could create a storyboard about a day in the life of their bug and present it to the group.

# Communication

We provide two types of communication: a classroom posting for students and visitors and a parent letter to be sent home. These can be found on the next two pages and on the accompanying CD-ROM.

# Bug Helpers Vocabulary Words

aphid

beetle

claws

dragonfly

ladybug

praying mantis

tarantula

waist

wasp

web

*PAVEd for Success: Building Vocabulary and Language Development in Young Learners,* by Claire E. Hamilton & Paula J. Schwanenflugel.

Dear Parents:

This week we will be focusing on vocabulary words for Bug Helpers. We will be reading stories and carrying out activities to help your child learn the meanings of these words. By pointing out examples of these words at home and in the community, you can help your child expand his or her vocabulary. This week's words (with simple definitions that children can understand) are as follows:

| | |
|---|---|
| **aphid** | a small green bug that lives on plants |
| **beetle** | a bug that eats dead things like fallen trees |
| **claws** | a sharp curved nail at the end of a leg |
| **dragonfly** | a bug with big wings that eats mosquitoes |
| **ladybug** | a small bug that's usually orange-red with black spots |
| **praying mantis** | a big green bug that catches bugs with its hands |
| **tarantula** | a large hairy spider |
| **waist** | the middle part of your body |
| **wasp** | a flying bug that stings and is usually brown |
| **web** | the thing that spiders make to trap food |

Please post this where you and your child can see it. Thanks!

Sincerely,

Your child's teacher

# Dental Health

## Vocabulary

| | |
|---|---|
| bacteria | gum |
| braces | hygienist |
| cavity | mouthwash |
| drill | saliva |
| floss | x ray |

## New VEhicles— N3C Vocabulary Introduction

### Initial Presentation

Find pictures for all vocabulary words listed below as well as the two known words paired with each vocabulary word. The known words should be in children's vocabularies. If not, substitute another from the set of pictures that your students are likely to know. In the large-group setting show all three pictures (the vocabulary word and the two known words) randomly to the children and ask them, "Which one is _____?" (insert vocabulary word). The children should be able to infer that the vocabulary word refers to the unknown picture among the three. If you wish, the quick definitions can be introduced then as well. All pictures are included in the accompanying CD-ROM.

| Vocabulary words | Known words |
|---|---|
| bacteria | chicken, dog |
| braces | brush, flower |
| cavity | bell, cake |
| drill | arm, banana |
| floss | cookie, fork |
| gum | sandwich, pumpkin |
| hygienist | dentist, teeth |
| mouthwash | toothbrush, hand |
| saliva | tongue, milk |
| x ray | present, doctor |

### Subsequent Presentation

After the initial presentation the pictures of the known words can be put away. The rest of the week, display only the pictures of the vocabulary words and say to children, "Show me _____" (insert vocabulary word) or "What's the word for this?" (point at picture).

## Quick Definitions

**bacteria**  little living things that we can't see; some are good and some are bad (like the ones that rot your teeth)

**braces**  wires that dentists use to straighten your teeth

**cavity**  a hole in your tooth that the dentist fixes

**drill**  what the dentist uses to fix a cavity

**floss**  a string used to clean between your teeth

**gum**  the pink stuff in your mouth that holds your teeth

**hygienist**  a person who helps the dentist with his patients

**mouthwash**  you swish it around your mouth to clean your teeth a little more

**saliva**  the wet, watery stuff in your mouth

**x ray**  a special picture doctors use to make sure your teeth or bones are okay

 ## CAR Quest

The following are questions that you can ask students about the story you are reading. We suggest reviewing the text beforehand and using sticky notes to mark appropriate places to pause for discussion. The questions are labeled according to the types described in Chapter 3.

### Books

Mayer, M. (2001). *Just going to the dentist.* New York: Penguin Group.

Katz, B. (1999). *Make way for tooth decay.* New York: Scholastic.

Page location describes the picture (illustration or photo) that relates to the individual CAR Quest question. Unknown vocabulary words are *italicized*.

### *Just Going to the Dentist*

Page location: Little Critter looks at the older child wearing *braces*

    **Relate:** Have you ever seen someone wearing *braces*?

    **Abstract:** How do you think *braces* help to straighten your teeth?

Page location: Mom, Little Critter, and the dentist look at the *x rays*.

    **Competence:** What are these *x rays* pictures of?

Page location: The dentist gets ready to give Little Critter a shot.

    **Abstract:** What do you think causes a *cavity*?

    **Relate:** Have you ever had a *cavity*?

Page location: The dentist *drills* Little Critter's tooth.

    **Competence:** What does the dentist have in his hand?

### *Make Way for Tooth Decay*

Page location: Brightly colored *bacteria* are having a party on the teeth.

    **Competence:** What do the *bacteria* look like in this picture?

    **Abstract:** In our book the *bacteria* look like they are misbehaving on the teeth. Why would they do that?

    **Relate:** What do you think the *bacteria* are like in your mouth?

**Page location:** Boy on skateboard spits in front of two girls

    **Competence:** What does *saliva* do?

**Page location:** Girl gets ready to *floss* her teeth.

    **Relate:** Has anyone ever *flossed* their teeth?

    **Abstract:** What do you think would happen if you never *flossed* your teeth?

## Building Bridges— Start 'em Up! Topic

Tell me what happened when you went to the dentist.

## New VEhicles— Extension Activities

### Activity 1: Polish the Tooth

**Materials:** Empty plastic water or soda bottles (cut off bottoms ahead of time), shaving cream (or suds from dish soap), toothbrushes, yarn or string, paper towels, brown and green washable markers

**Description:** Give each group a "tooth" (the end of the plastic bottle). Have each child draw a *cavity* by drawing a line with a brown marker and some *bacteria*, which they should make as dots with a green marker. Cover the tooth with shaving cream. Have the children take turns brushing with the toothbrush, *flossing* with the yarn, and polishing with the cloth until their tooth is *cavity* and *bacteria* free. Water could be used to demonstrate *mouthwash* or *saliva*. Pink clay might also be added to show *gums*.

### Activity 2: Examine the X Ray

**Materials:** Pictures of *x rays* (use Google Images), magnifying glass (optional)

**Description:** Choose a child to be the dentist. Put a chair in the center of the circle for the patient. Distribute the *x rays* to the children, including the ones of teeth. Ask each child to go up to the dentist.

Have the dentist practice a greeting: "Hi, Jevon. Can I examine your teeth?"

Have the child show the *x ray* and say, "This is my *x ray;* can you help me?"

Now it is the dentist's turn to say either "Yes, it looks like you have healthy teeth" or "Yes, it looks like you have a *cavity*/need to *floss*/have too much *bacteria*/need *braces* and I need my *hygienist,*" and so forth, using the vocabulary.

# Communication

We provide two types of communication: a classroom posting for students and visitors and a parent letter to be sent home. These are on the next two pages and on the accompanying CD-ROM.

# Dental Health Vocabulary Words

bacteria

braces

cavity

drill

floss

gum

hygienist

mouthwash

saliva

x ray

Dear Parents,

This week we will be focusing on vocabulary words for Dental Health. We will be reading stories and carrying out activities to help your child learn the meanings of these words. By pointing out examples of these words at home and in the community, you can help your child expand his or her vocabulary. This week's words (with simple definitions that children can understand) are as follows:

| | |
|---|---|
| **bacteria** | little living things that we can't see; some are good and some are bad (like the ones that rot your teeth) |
| **braces** | wires that dentists use to straighten your teeth |
| **cavity** | a hole in your tooth that the dentist fixes |
| **drill** | what the dentist uses to fix a cavity |
| **floss** | a string used to clean between your teeth |
| **gum** | the pink stuff in your mouth that holds your teeth |
| **hygienist** | a person who helps the dentist with his patients |
| **mouthwash** | you swish it around your mouth to clean your teeth a little more |
| **saliva** | the wet, watery stuff in your mouth |
| **x ray** | a special picture doctors use to make sure your teeth or bones are okay |

Please post this where you and your child can see it. Thanks!

Sincerely,

Your child's teacher

UNIT

**4** **Feelings**

- - - - - - - - - - - - - - - - - - - - - - - - - - - - - - - - - - - - - - - - - - - - - - - - - - - - -

## Vocabulary

| | |
|---|---|
| angry | excited |
| bored | exhausted |
| confused | frustrated |
| disappointed | proud |
| disgusted | shy |

# New VEhicles—
# N3C Vocabulary Introduction

## Initial Presentation

Find pictures for all vocabulary words listed below as well as the two known words paired with each vocabulary word. The known words should be in children's vocabularies. If not, substitute another from the set of pictures that your students are likely to know. In the large-group setting show all three pictures (the vocabulary word and the two known words) randomly to the children and ask them, "Which one is _____?" (insert vocabulary word). The children should be able to infer that the vocabulary word refers to the unknown picture among the three. If you wish, the quick definitions can be introduced then as well. All pictures are included in the accompanying CD-ROM.

| Vocabulary words | Known words |
|---|---|
| angry | teeth, doctor |
| bored | bib, pants |
| confused | tree, mad |
| disappointed | coat, glasses |
| disgusted | cookie, happy |
| excited | cow, sad |
| exhausted | saw, happy |
| frustrated | policeman, sad |
| proud | teacher, mad |
| shy | drum, mad |

## Subsequent Presentation

After the initial presentation the pictures of the known words can be put away. The rest of the week, display only the pictures of the vocabulary words and say to children, "Show me _____" (insert vocabulary word) or "What's the word for this?" (point at picture).

# Quick Definitions

**angry**    you are angry when someone does something wrong to you

**bored**    when you are tired of doing something

**confused**    you are confused when you can't figure out what to do

**disappointed**    you are disappointed when something you want doesn't happen

**disgusted**    you are disgusted when something smells so bad that it makes you kind of sick

**excited**    you are excited when something fun is going to happen, like a field trip

**exhausted**    you are exhausted when you are very, very tired

**frustrated**    you feel frustrated when you can't do something you are trying to do, like when you can't tie your shoelaces

**proud**    you feel proud when you do something very well

**shy**    you are shy when you are afraid to join in because you don't know if the other kids will like you

 # CAR Quest

The following are questions that you can ask students about the story you are reading. We suggest reviewing the text beforehand and using sticky notes to mark appropriate places to pause for discussion. The questions are labeled according to the types described in Chapter 3.

## Books

Cain, J. (2000). *The way I feel*. Seattle: Parenting Press.

Bang, M. (1999). *When Sophie gets angry—really, really angry…*. New York: Blue Sky Press.

Page location describes the picture (illustration or photo) that relates to the individual CAR Quest question. Unknown vocabulary words are *italicized*.

### *The Way I Feel*

**Page location:** Girl tries to tie her shoe

   **Relate:** When was the last time you felt *frustrated*?

   **Abstract:** Why do you think this girl is *frustrated*?

**Page location:** Girl hides behind her mother

   **Competence:** How can you tell that she is *shy*?

   **Relate:** Have you ever been *shy* before? What happened?

**Page location:** *Bored* boy sits on chair

   **Abstract:** Why do think this boy is *bored*?

   **Competence:** Where is this boy sitting while he is *bored*?

### *When Sophie Gets Angry—Really, Really Angry…*

**Page location:** The cat watches Sophie stamp her feet.

   **Competence:** What is Sophie doing in this picture?

   **Relate:** Have you ever been *angry* before? What happened?

   **Abstract:** Can you think of something that would make you *angry*?

**Page location:** Sophie walks head-down through the trees. (She looks *disappointed*, doesn't she?)

   **Relate:** Can you talk about a time when you were *disappointed* about something?

   **Abstract:** Why do you think Sophie is *disappointed*?

**Page location:** Sophie sits in a tree and looks at the ocean.

   **Competence:** What is this *exhausted* little girl doing in this picture?

# Building Bridges— Start 'em Up! Topic

This morning I was excited because I (fill in something you were excited about). What feelings did you have this morning before you came to school?

# New VEhicles— Extension Activities

## Activity 1: Acting out Emotions

**Materials:** Hand mirror (or full-length mirror if you have it)

**Description:** Have the children take turns acting out the target vocabulary emotions in the mirror. Have partners help each other make their faces look even closer to the emotion term.

## Activity 2: Feelings Collage

**Materials:** Paper, magazines and newspapers, glue

**Description:** Give your children magazines and newspapers. Have them cut out people who are showing different emotions. Have them separate these cut-outs based on the emotion (positive, negative, neutral) and then make a collage with different sides of the paper representing different emotions, *or* simply let children sort the pictures based on the emotions they perceive.

# Communication

We provide two types of communication: a classroom posting for students and visitors and a parent letter to be sent home. These are on the next two pages and on the accompanying CD-ROM.

# Feelings Vocabulary Words

angry

bored

confused

disappointed

disgusted

excited

exhausted

frustrated

proud

shy

Dear Parents:

This week we will be focusing on vocabulary words for Feelings. We will be reading stories and carrying out activities to help your child learn the meanings of these words. By pointing out examples of these words at home and in the community, you can help your child expand his or her vocabulary. This week's words (with simple definitions that children can understand) are as follows:

| | |
|---|---|
| angry | you are angry when someone does something wrong to you |
| bored | when you are tired of doing something |
| confused | you are confused when you can't figure out what to do |
| disappointed | you are disappointed when something you want doesn't happen |
| disgusted | you are disgusted when something smells so bad that it makes you kind of sick |
| excited | you are excited when something fun is going to happen, like a field trip |
| exhausted | you are exhausted when you are very, very tired |
| frustrated | you feel frustrated when you can't do something you are trying to do, like when you can't tie your shoelaces |
| proud | you feel proud when you do something very well |
| shy | you are shy when you are afraid to join in because you don't know if the other kids will like you |

Please post this where you and your child can see it. Thanks!

Sincerely,

Your child's teacher

UNIT

5 Gardening

## Vocabulary

| | |
|---|---|
| blackberry | radish |
| cucumber | rake |
| garden | root |
| hoe | seeds |
| plant | soil |

## New VEhicles— N3C Vocabulary Introduction

### Initial Presentation

Find pictures for all vocabulary words listed below as well as the two known words paired with each vocabulary word. The known words should be in children's vocabularies. If not, substitute another from the set of pictures that your students are likely to know. In the large-group setting show all three pictures (the vocabulary word and the two known words) randomly to the children and ask them, "Which one is _____?" (insert vocabulary word). The children should be able to infer that the vocabulary word refers to the unknown picture among the three. If you wish, the quick definitions can be introduced then as well. All pictures are included in the accompanying CD-ROM.

| Vocabulary words | Known words |
|---|---|
| blackberry | banana, apple |
| cucumber | bread, cake |
| garden | sandwich, leaf |
| hoe | present, fork |
| plant | sock, hat |
| radish | cheese, pumpkin |
| rake | bag, shirt |
| root | tree, hammer |
| seeds | ring, egg |
| soil | snowman, mouse |

### Subsequent Presentation

After the initial presentation the pictures of the known words can be put away. The rest of the week, display only the pictures of the vocabulary words and say to the children, "Show me _____" (insert vocabulary word) or "What's the word for this?" (point at picture).

# Quick Definitions

**blackberry**   a dark fruit growing on a bush

**cucumber**   a long green fruit growing on a vine, eaten in salads

**garden**   a place where someone grows fruits, vegetables, or flowers

**hoe**   a tool used to break up the dirt before planting seeds

**plant**   a green thing growing in the ground

**radish**   a red root that some people eat; very bitter

**rake**   a tool used to clear the ground for a garden

**root**   the part of the plant that grows down into the dirt

**seeds**   what we put in the ground so that a plant can grow from them

**soil**   another word for dirt

 # CAR Quest

The following are questions that you can ask students about the story you are reading. We suggest reviewing the text beforehand and using sticky notes to mark appropriate places to pause for discussion. The questions are labeled according to the types described in Chapter 3.

## Books

Potter, B. (2004). *The tale of Peter Rabbit.* New York: Grosset & Dunlap.

Stewart, S. (2000). *The gardener.* New York: Farrar, Straus and Giroux.

Page location describes the picture (illustration or photo) that relates to the individual CAR Quest question. Unknown vocabulary words are *italicized.*

### *The Tale of Peter Rabbit*

**Page location:** Three bunnies collect *blackberries* in a basket.

   **Competence:** Do you see the rabbits picking the little *blackberries*? Which ones are the *blackberries*? Can you point to them?

**Page location:** Peter Rabbit climbs under the *garden* fence.

   **Relate:** Has anyone ever eaten a *radish*? What does it taste like?

**Page location:** Mr. McGregor chases Peter Rabbit through the *garden.*

   **Relate:** Who likes to eat *cucumbers*? Does anyone like them in salad?

   **Abstract:** Why shouldn't Mr. McGregor wave the *rake* up in the air like that?

**Page location:** Peter Rabbit watches Mr. McGregor *hoe* the *garden.*

   **Competence:** What is Mr. McGregor using the *hoe* for?

   **Abstract:** Why do you think Peter is afraid of Mr. McGregor's *hoe*?

### *The Gardener*

**Page location:** Letter written September 3rd

   **Abstract:** Let's go back to the opening picture in the book. What makes this a *garden*?

   **Relate:** Does anyone have a *garden* at home? What do you grow there?

**Page location:** Letter written September 4th

Competence: Can you show me the *seeds* in the picture? They are in these envelopes.

Abstract: She is going to stay in a city for a while. Do you think she should take her *seeds* to *plant* a *garden* there?

Relate: Have you ever *planted seeds* before?

Competence: What do people do with *seeds*?

## Building Bridges— Start 'em Up! Topic

If you had a *garden*, what would you grow in it?

## New VEhicles— Extension Activities

### Activity 1: Two Ways to Plant Bean Seeds

**Materials:** Two lima bean *seeds* per student, zip-top bags (one per student), paper towels, egg cartons sliced up or paper cups, *soil*, paper, pencil

**Description:** Each student will be asked to *plant* a seed in the *soil* after germinating it in a closed, wet zip-top bag for a day or so. Afterward the children will draw what they think their *plant* will grow into and place it in their *garden*. Children should be asked what kind of tools they would need (e.g., *rake, hoe*) and what else they might want to grow (e.g., *blackberries, radishes, cucumbers*).

### Activity 2: Create Your Own Garden

**Materials:** Paper, crayons, vocabulary pictures as models

**Description:** Children will decide what they want to *plant* in their *garden* and what tools they will use to create the *garden*. They will draw a picture of it and share it with the other children in the group.

## Communication

We provide two types of communication: a classroom posting for students and visitors and a parent letter to be sent home. These are on the next two pages and on the accompanying CD-ROM.

# Gardening Vocabulary Words

blackberry

cucumber

garden

hoe

plant

radish

rake

root

seeds

soil

Dear Parents,

This week we will be focusing on vocabulary words for Gardening. We will be reading stories and carrying out activities to help your child learn the meanings of these words. By pointing out examples of these words at home and in the community, you can help your child expand his or her vocabulary. This week's words (with simple definitions that children can understand) are as follows:

| | |
|---|---|
| blackberry | a dark fruit growing on a bush |
| cucumber | a long green fruit growing on a vine, eaten in salads |
| garden | a place where someone grows fruits, vegetables, or flowers |
| hoe | a tool used to break up the dirt before planting seeds |
| plant | a green thing growing in the ground |
| radish | a red root that some people eat; very bitter |
| rake | a tool used to clear the ground for a garden |
| root | the part of the plant that grows down into the dirt |
| seeds | what we put in the ground so that a plant can grow from them |
| soil | another word for dirt |

Please post this where you and your child can see it. Thanks!

Sincerely,

Your child's teacher

UNIT
**6**
# Living in the Earth
## Worms and Pill Bugs

- - - - - - - - - - - - - - - - - - - - - - - - - - - - - - - - - - - - - - - - - - - - - - - - -

## Vocabulary

| | |
|---|---|
| antennae | passageway |
| ants | pill bug |
| chipmunk | shell |
| concrete | shovel |
| earthworm | shrimp |

## New VEhicles—
## N3C Vocabulary Introduction

### Initial Presentation

Find pictures for all vocabulary words listed below as well as the two known words paired with each vocabulary word. The known words should be in children's vocabularies. If not, substitute another from the set of pictures that your students are likely to know. In the large-group setting show all three pictures (the vocabulary word and the two known words) randomly to the children and ask them, "Which one is _____?" (insert vocabulary word). The children should be able to infer that the vocabulary word refers to the unknown picture among the three. If you wish, the quick definitions can be introduced then as well. All pictures are included in the accompanying CD-ROM.

| Vocabulary words | Known words |
|---|---|
| antennae | boot, frog |
| ants | baseball, bell |
| chipmunk | bird, dinosaur |
| concrete | tree, leaf |
| earthworm | bottle, foot |
| passageway | train, house |
| pill bug | dress, egg |
| shell | shoe, shirt |
| shovel | scissors, pencil |
| shrimp | cow, frog |

### Subsequent Presentation

After the initial presentation the pictures of the known words can be put away. The rest of the week, display only the pictures of the vocabulary words and say to children, "Show me _____" (insert vocabulary word) or "What's the word for this?" (point at picture).

# Quick Definitions

**antennae**   things on a bug's head that tell it where to go

**ants**   a small bug that eats your food

**chipmunk**   a small striped squirrel

**concrete**   the hard stuff that sidewalks and basements are usually made of

**earthworm**   a snakelike bug that lives in the ground

**passageway**   a type of hall found underground or between rooms or buildings

**pill bug**   a small animal with a shell that can curl into a ball; lives on land

**shell**   the hard outside of bugs and some fish

**shovel**   you use it to dig

**shrimp**   a small animal living on the bottom of the sea

# CAR Quest

The following are questions that you can ask students about the story you are reading. We suggest reviewing the text beforehand and using sticky notes to mark appropriate places to pause for discussion. The questions are labeled according to the types described in Chapter 3.

## Books

Glaser, L. (1992). *Wonderful worms*. New York: Scholastic.

Tokuda, Y. (2006). *I'm a pill bug*. San Diego: Kane/Miller.

Page location describes the picture (illustration or photo) that relates to the individual CAR Quest question. Unknown vocabulary words are *italicized*.

### Wonderful Worms

**Page location:** First picture, barefoot child holds *earthworm*

   **Competence:** Who can point to the *earthworms*? How many are there?

   **Relate:** Have you ever seen an *earthworm* on the ground after it rains?

**Page location:** Two sneakers stand above *chipmunk* and *earthworms*

   **Competence:** Can you see the *chipmunk* in a burrow? What does he have hidden away there?

   **Abstract:** Why does the *chipmunk* go into the burrow?

**Page location:** Child pokes finger into hole made by *earthworm*

   **Abstract:** How is the *earthworm* moving through the *passageway*?

   **Relate:** Can you dig a *passageway* with a *shovel*?

### I'm a Pill Bug

**Page location:** *Ants* and *pill bugs* meet.

   **Abstract:** Why do you think the *ant* is scary to the *pill bug*?

   **Relate:** Is anyone here scared of *ants*?

Page location: An *ant* approaches a *pill bug* rolled into a ball.

    Abstract: Can you think of other animals that use *shells* for protection? (clams, turtles, *shrimp*, lobsters, beetles, snails)

Page location: Picture of a crab and *shrimp*

    Competence: Who has more legs, the *pill bug* or the *ant*?

    Competence: How do crabs, *shrimp* and *pill bugs* look alike?

Page location: *Pill bugs* move amongst dirt, fall leaves, and stones.

    Relate: Would you like to eat *concrete* or stones?

# Building Bridges—
# Start 'em Up! Topic

Would you rather be an *ant*, a *pill bug*, or a *shrimp*? Why?

# New VEhicles—
# Extension Activities

## Activity 1: Earthworm Art Activity

**Materials:** Construction paper, colored pens

**Description:** Talk about how *earthworms* always live underground in the *soil*. As they eat they create *passageways* and tunnels and move along. Sometimes they come across roots. Encourage your students to draw *earthworms* traveling in *passageways* and through tunnels in between roots. If they like they can add a tunnel leading to a burrow with a *chipmunk* curled up inside. Students could also develop creative stories about their art using the target vocabulary (Are there *ants* in the picture? What happens if the *earthworm* hits a stone?).

## Activity 2: Stories About Living in the Earth

**Materials:** Construction paper, colored pens/markers/crayons

**Description:** Students will draw a storyboard about the adventures of a *pill bug*, *earthworm*, *chipmunk*, and *ant*. Time for sharing should be allotted.

# Communication

We provide two types of communication: a classroom posting for students and visitors and a parent letter to be sent home. These are on the next two pages and on the accompanying CD-ROM.

# Living in the Earth: Worms and Pill Bugs Vocabulary Words

antennae

ants

chipmunk

concrete

earthworm

passageway

pill bug

shell

shovel

shrimp

Dear Parents:

This week we will be focusing on vocabulary words for Living in the Earth: Worms and Pill Bugs. We will be reading stories and carrying out activities to help your child learn the meanings of these words. By pointing out examples of these words at home and in the community, you can help your child expand his or her vocabulary. This week's words (with simple definitions that children can understand) are as follows:

| | |
|---|---|
| **antennae** | things on a bug's head that tell it where to go |
| **ants** | small bugs that eat your food |
| **chipmunk** | a small striped squirrel |
| **concrete** | the hard stuff that sidewalks and basements are usually made of |
| **earthworm** | a snakelike bug that lives in the ground |
| **passageway** | a type of hall found underground or between rooms or buildings |
| **pill bug** | a small animal with a shell that can curl into a ball; lives on land |
| **shell** | the hard outside of bugs and some fish |
| **shovel** | you use it to dig |
| **shrimp** | a small animal living on the bottom of the sea |

Please post this where you and your child can see it. Thanks!

Sincerely,

Your child's teacher

UNIT

**7** **Magnets**

Vocabulary

| | |
|---|---|
| attract | paper clip |
| cork | penny |
| iron | repel |
| magnet | tack |
| needle | twig |

## New VEhicles— N3C Vocabulary Introduction

### Initial Presentation

Find pictures for all vocabulary words listed below as well as the two known words paired with each vocabulary word. The known words should be in children's vocabularies. If not, substitute another from the set of pictures that your students are likely to know. In the large-group setting, show all three pictures (the vocabulary word and the two known words) randomly to the children and ask them, "Which one is _____?" (insert vocabulary word). The children should be able to infer that the vocabulary word refers to the unknown picture among the three. If you wish, the quick definitions can be introduced then as well. All pictures are included in the accompanying CD-ROM.

| Vocabulary words | Known words |
|---|---|
| attract | cookie, guitar |
| cork | ball, brush |
| iron | plane, key |
| magnet | saw, fridge |
| needle | bottle, toothbrush |
| paper clip | ring, guitar |
| penny | ring, eye |
| repel | couch, jump |
| tack | window, drum |
| twig | spoon, pencil |

### Subsequent Presentation

After the initial presentation the pictures of the known words can be put away. The rest of the week, display only the pictures of the vocabulary words and say to children, "Show me _____" (insert vocabulary word) or "What's the word for this?" (point at picture).

## Quick Definitions

**attract**   when two things pull together

**cork**   you put it in the top of a bottle

**iron**   a strong, hard metal used to make such things as gates and railings

**magnet**   something that some metals stick to

**needle**   something you sew with or a way to point

**paper clip**   it holds pieces of paper together

**penny**   a copper coin that is worth one cent

**repel**   to push something away

**tack**   a small nail-like thing that you use to hang things up with

**twig**   a small thin piece of a tree or bush

## CAR Quest

The following are questions that you can ask students about the story you are reading. We suggest reviewing the text beforehand and using sticky notes to mark appropriate places to pause for discussion. The questions are labeled according to the types described in Chapter 3.

### Books

Branley, F. (1996). *What makes a magnet?* New York: HarperCollins.

Rosinsky, N. (2003). *Magnets: Pulling together, pushing apart.* Minneapolis, MN: Picture Window Books.

Page location describes the picture (illustration or photo) that relates to the individual CAR Quest question. Unknown vocabulary words are *italicized*.

### *What Makes a Magnet?*

**Page location:** Girl tosses coins, sticks, paper and other objects into a box

    **Abstract:** Do you think a *magnet* will *attract* a *penny*?

**Page location:** Picture illustrates different types of *magnets*

    **Competence:** How many *magnets* are on the page?

    **Relate:** What kind of *magnets* do you have in your home?

    **Relate:** Do we have any *magnets* in our classroom?

    **Abstract:** How can a *magnet* on your refrigerator help out?

**Page location:** Step 1 in making a compass

    **Competence:** What are *needles* usually used for?

### *Magnets: Pulling Together, Pushing Apart*

**Page location:** Girl holds a puppet while boy uses *magnet* to attract two nails and two *paper clips*

    **Relate:** Can anyone point to a *paper clip* in the classroom?

    **Abstract:** How do we use *paper clips*?

**Page location:** A boy and a girl hold the north pole of two *magnets* together.

   **Competence:** When the *magnets repel* each other, what do the *magnets* do?

**Page location:** Girl examines the attraction between the north and south poles of *two magnets*

   **Competence:** When the *magnets attract* each other, what do the *magnets* do?

**Page location:** Girl in the woods inspects her compass

   **Relate:** Have you ever used a *needle* for anything? What was it?

   **Abstract:** What is the *needle* on the compass used for?

# Building Bridges—
# Start 'em Up! Topic

The last time I used a *paper clip*, it wasn't to find direction. I used it to hold pieces of paper together. The same with *needles*—I used one to sew a button on my sweater. How do you use things like *needles, paper clips, magnets,* and *tacks* in your home?

# New VEhicles—
# Extension Activities

## Activity 1: Magnetic or Not?

**Materials:** *Magnet, needle, penny, twig, tack, iron* material of any sort, *cork, paper clip*

**Description:** The teacher will ask students to use their *magnets* to decide which materials are magnetic. The instructor should call out the item and ask students to respond with a yes or no depending on whether or not the item is magnetic.

## Activity 2: Do We Attract, Repel, or Do Nothing Contra Dance?

**Materials:** Vocabulary pictures provided, several copies of the *magnet* picture with a + (plus) or a – (minus) written on it in large print

**Description:** Every child gets a picture. Students line up in two lines facing one another. In a standard contra dance, the pair on the end of the line gets together and dances down the aisle and returns to the line. In this dance, children who have pictures that *attract* each other will hold hands and shuffle down the aisle. Children who *repel* each other will shuffle down back to back. Children whose items do nothing simply walk side by side without touching.

# Communication

We provide two types of communication: a classroom posting for students and visitors and a parent letter to be sent home. These are found on the next two pages and on the accompanying CD-ROM.

# Magnets Vocabulary Words

attract

cork

iron

magnet

needle

paper clip

penny

repel

tack

twig

Dear Parents:

This week we will be focusing on vocabulary words for Magnets. We will be reading stories and carrying out activities to help your child learn the meanings of these words. By pointing out examples of these words at home and in the community, you can help your child expand his or her vocabulary. This week's words (with simple definitions that children can understand) are as follows:

| | |
|---|---|
| **attract** | when two things pull together |
| **cork** | you put it in the top of a bottle |
| **iron** | a strong, hard metal used to make such things as gates and railings |
| **magnet** | something that some metals stick to |
| **needle** | something you sew with or a way to point |
| **paper clip** | it holds pieces of paper together |
| **penny** | a copper coin that is worth one cent |
| **repel** | to push something away |
| **tack** | a small nail-like thing that you use to hang things up with |
| **twig** | a small thin piece of a tree or bush |

Please post this where you and your child can see it. Thanks!

Sincerely,

Your child's teacher

UNIT

# 8 Outer Space

## Vocabulary

| | |
|---|---|
| appear | moon |
| bright | rise |
| disappear | sink |
| dusk | sliver |
| Earth | star |

## New VEhicles— N3C Vocabulary Introduction

### Initial Presentation

Find pictures for all vocabulary words listed below as well as the two known words paired with each vocabulary word. The known words should be in children's vocabularies. If not, substitute another from the set of pictures that your students are likely to know. In the large-group setting show all three pictures (the vocabulary word and the two known words) randomly to the children and ask them, "Which one is _____?" (insert vocabulary word). The children should be able to infer that the vocabulary word refers to the unknown picture among the three. If you wish, the quick definitions can be introduced then as well. All pictures are included in the accompanying CD-ROM.

| Vocabulary words | Known words |
|---|---|
| appear | butterfly, policeman |
| bright | bridge, pants |
| disappear | bib, flag |
| dusk | rain, lamp |
| Earth | rain, flag |
| moon | corn, heart |
| rise | run, jump |
| sink | table, toilet |
| sliver | pencil, mouse |
| star | sun, heart |

### Subsequent Presentation

After the initial presentation the pictures of the known words can be put away. The rest of the week, display only the pictures of the vocabulary words and say to children, "Show me _____" (insert vocabulary word) or "What's the word for this?" (point at picture).

# Quick Definitions

**appear**    to come out where you can see it

**bright**    so much light you have to wear sunglasses

**disappear**    to go away where you can't see it

**dusk**    the time of day when it is almost dark outside

**Earth**    it's where everyone in the whole world lives

**moon**    the round white ball that you see in the sky at night

**rise**    to go up

**sink**    to go down

**sliver**    a small skinny piece of something

**star**    small white dots you see in the sky at night

 # CAR Quest

The following are questions that you can ask students about the story you are reading. We suggest reviewing the text beforehand and using sticky notes to mark appropriate places to pause for discussion. The questions are labeled according to the types described in Chapter 3.

## Books

Carle, E. (1986). *Papa, please get the moon for me.* New York: Simon & Schuster Books for Young Readers.

Sherman, J. (2004). *Sunshine: A book about sunlight.* Minneapolis, MN: Picture Window Books.

Page location describes the picture (illustration or photo) that relates to the individual CAR Quest question. Unknown vocabulary words are *italicized*.

### Papa, Please Get the Moon for Me

**Page location:** Monica sits on her father's shoulders and reaches toward the *moon*.

   **Competence:**  What color is the *moon*?

   **Relate:** How does this *moon* look like the one you see out of your window? How does it look different?

   **Abstract:**  Do you think if you got a big enough ladder you could touch the *moon*?

**Page location:** Monica looks out her window at the *sliver* of the *moon*.

   **Competence:**  Where is the *sliver* of the *moon*?

   **Relate:** Have you ever seen the *moon* look like a *sliver*? When was it?

   **Abstract:**  Why do you think the *moon* is sometimes full and sometimes looks like a *sliver*?

### Sunshine: A Book About Sunlight

**Page location:** Picture shows the Earth rotating around the giant sun.

   **Competence:** Where do you see *stars*?

   **Abstract:** The sun, our *star*, seems to *rise* in the morning. What else can you think of that *rises*?

**Page location:** The sun sets and the sky above a house and tree are orange.

> **Relate:** What do you usually do at *dusk*?

> **Abstract:** What does it mean that the sun *appears* to set at *dusk*?

**Page location:** A full *moon* shines over the water.

> **Competence:** What color is the *moon* at night?

**Page location:** The sun *rises* between the mountains.

> **Relate:** Where do you usually go when the sun *appears* and another day begins?

# Building Bridges—
# Start 'em Up! Topic

What were you doing at *dusk* yesterday? Was there a *moon* last night? Did anyone notice what it looked like?

# New VEhicles—
# Extension Activities

## Activity 1: Clock Activity

**Materials:** Paper plates; crayons; markers; colored pencils; small pictures of *bright, moon, dusk, dawn*

**Description:** Take two paper plates and have children write *Morning* on one and *Evening* on the other. Have them draw the numbers of an analog clock on the edges of the plates. On the morning plate have them glue *dawn* at 6 a.m. and *bright* at noon; on the evening plate have them glue *dusk* at 6 p.m. and *moon* at midnight. Staple the back sides of the clock together.

## Activity 2: Let's Pretend to Be the Earth, Sun, and Moon

**Materials:** Strong flashlight, dark classroom

**Description:** Turn off the classroom lights and darken the classroom as much as is feasible. One student in the group holds the flashlight and is the sun. Another student in the group is the *Earth*. Another student is the *moon*. The student who is the *Earth* turns around. When the flashlight is shining on his or her face, it is day and it is *bright*. When he or she has turned halfway around it is *dusk* and daylight is *disappearing*. When the light is on his or her back it is night. The student who is the *moon* walks around the *Earth*. When the child is on the flashlight side of the *Earth*, the *moon* is full. When the *moon* walks behind the *Earth*, it is a *sliver* and is *disappearing*. Have students talk about what is happening using *sliver, Earth, disappear, dusk, bright,* and *appear*.

# Communication

We provide two types of communication: a classroom posting for students and visitors and a parent letter to be sent home. These are on the next two pages and on the accompanying CD-ROM.

# Outer Space Vocabulary Words

appear

bright

disappear

dusk

Earth

moon

rise

sink

sliver

star

Dear Parents:

This week we will be focusing on vocabulary words for Outer Space. We will be reading stories and carrying out activities to help your child learn the meanings of these words. By pointing out examples of these words at home and in the community, you can help your child expand his or her vocabulary. This week's words (with simple definitions that children can understand) are as follows:

| | |
|---|---|
| appear | to come out where you can see it |
| bright | so much light you have to wear sunglasses |
| disappear | to go away where you can't see it |
| dusk | the time of day when it is almost dark outside |
| Earth | it's where everyone in the whole world lives |
| moon | the round white ball that you see in the sky at night |
| rise | to go up |
| sink | to go down |
| sliver | a small skinny piece of something |
| star | small white dot you see in the sky at night |

Please post this where you and your child can see it. Thanks!

Sincerely,

Your child's teacher

# Recycling and the Environment

## Vocabulary

| | |
|---|---|
| barge | picnic |
| compost | poison |
| junkyard | recycle bin |
| landfill | sand dune |
| litter | tide pool |

## New VEhicles— N3C Vocabulary Introduction

### Initial Presentation

Find pictures for all vocabulary words listed below as well as the two known words paired with each vocabulary word. The known words should be in children's vocabularies. If not, substitute another from the set of pictures that your students are likely to know. In the large-group setting show all three pictures (the vocabulary word and the two known words) randomly to the children and ask them, "Which one is _____?" (insert vocabulary word). The children should be able to infer that the vocabulary word refers to the unknown picture among the three. If you wish, the quick definitions can be introduced then as well. All pictures are included in the accompanying CD-ROM.

| Vocabulary word | Known words |
|---|---|
| barge | bridge, run |
| compost | hat, flag |
| junkyard | present, hamburger |
| landfill | road, leaf |
| litter | corn, mouse |
| picnic | pumpkin, mouth |
| poison | cat, horse |
| recycle bin | present, fridge |
| sand dune | tree, horse |
| tide pool | square, frog |

### Subsequent Presentation

After the initial presentation the pictures of the known words can be put away. The rest of the week, display only the pictures of the vocabulary words and say to children, "Show me _____" (insert vocabulary word) or "What's the word for this?" (point at picture).

# Quick Definitions

**barge**   a flat boat that carries heavy things

**compost**   a pile of old food and leaves that turns into dirt

**junkyard**   a place where old things are sold for their parts

**landfill**   where trash is taken

**litter**   trash thrown out on the ground—not in a trash can

**picnic**   having a meal outside

**poison**   something that can make you sick if you eat or breathe it

**recycle bin**   a place to put garbage so it can be turned into something else

**sand dune**   a big hill of sand that protects the land from the ocean

**tide pool**   a pool of water left on the beach

 # CAR Quest

The following are questions that you can ask students about the story you are reading. We suggest reviewing the text beforehand and using sticky notes to mark appropriate places to pause for discussion. The questions are labeled according to the types described in Chapter 3.

## Books

Green, J. (2002). *Why should I protect nature?* New York: Barron's.

Showers, P. (1994). *Where does the garbage go?* New York: Harper Trophy.

Page location describes the picture (illustration or photo) that relates to the individual CAR Quest question. Unknown vocabulary words are *italicized*.

### Why Should I Protect Nature?

**Page location:** The teacher and the children look at the *tide pool*.

   **Abstract:** What kinds of things do you think they found in the *tide pools*?

   **Relate:** Have you ever seen a *tide pool*?

**Page location:** The teacher and children have a *picnic* in the woods.

   **Competence:** Where will the children have their *picnic*?

   **Relate:** What foods would you pack for a *picnic*?

**Page location:** People throw *litter* out of the car windows.

   **Competence:** What does the *litter* look like?

   **Abstract:** What problems can *litter* cause?

### Where Does the Garbage Go?

**Page location:** A tugboat pulls a *barge* full of trash.

   **Competence:** Can you point to the *barge*? What's the *barge* carrying?

**Page location:** Three children play on the *sand dune*.

   **Abstract:** Why would it be bad for the waste and *litter* to float back to the beach?

**Page location:** A teacher and children watch the trucks in the *landfill*.

    **Competence:** How is the bulldozer spreading out the waste?

    **Relate:** Has anyone ever seen a *landfill*?

    **Abstract:** What kinds of things might you find in a dump or *landfill*?

**Page location:** A boy carries newspapers to the *recycle bin* at the curb.

    **Relate:** Have you ever used a *recycle bin*?

# Building Bridges—
# Start 'em Up! Topic

How do you help your parents recycle? How do you help keep our environment clean?

# New VEhicles—
# Extension Activities

## Activity 1: Let's Start Recycling

**Materials:** Boxes labeled *recycling, landfill, compost,* and *junkyard;* pictures of items that go into one of these boxes

**Description:** Tell children what each bin is for: the *recycling,* the *landfill,* and the *compost.* Have children put the picture cards with the correct bin. Have them talk with one another about why they made the decisions they made.

## Activity 2: Clean Picnic or Not

**Materials:** Paper, crayons

**Description:** Have children pretend they are going for a *picnic* at the beach (*tide pool, sand dune, barge* could all be included). Children should draw two pictures: one in which they decide to pick up their *litter* after their *picnic* and the other in which they do not. Have them discuss what would happen to the sea animals if they left their *litter* behind.

# Communication

We provide two types of communication: a classroom posting for students and visitors and a parent letter to be sent home. These are on the next two pages and on the accompanying CD-ROM.

# Recycling and the Environment Vocabulary Words

barge

compost

junkyard

landfill

litter

picnic

poison

recycle bin

sand dune

tide pool

Dear Parents:

This week we will be focusing on vocabulary words for Recycling and the Environment. We will be reading stories and carrying out activities to help your child learn the meanings of these words. By pointing out examples of these words at home and in the community, you can help your child expand his or her vocabulary. This week's words (with simple definitions that children can understand) are as follows:

| | |
|---|---|
| **barge** | a flat boat that carries heavy things |
| **compost** | a pile of old food and leaves that turns into dirt |
| **junkyard** | a place where old things are sold for their parts |
| **landfill** | where trash is taken |
| **litter** | trash thrown out on the ground—not in a trash can |
| **picnic** | having a meal outside |
| **poison** | something that can make you sick if you eat or breathe it |
| **recycle bin** | a place to put garbage so it can be turned into something else |
| **sand dune** | a big hill of sand that protects the land from the ocean |
| **tide pool** | a pool of water left on the beach |

Please post this where you and your child can see it. Thanks!

Sincerely,

Your child's teacher

UNIT

**10**
# Solids, Liquids, and Gases

------------------------------------------------------------

## Vocabulary

| | |
|---|---|
| boil | liquid |
| burner | melt |
| candle | plastic |
| container | steam |
| exhaust | temperature |

## New VEhicles— N3C Vocabulary Introduction

### Initial Presentation

Find pictures for all vocabulary words listed below as well as the two known words paired with each vocabulary word. The known words should be in children's vocabularies. If not, substitute another from the set of pictures that your students are likely to know. In the large-group setting show all three pictures (the vocabulary word and the two known words) randomly to the children and ask them, "Which one is _____?" (insert vocabulary word). The children should be able to infer that the vocabulary word refers to the unknown picture among the three. If you wish, the quick definitions can be introduced then as well. All pictures are included in the accompanying CD-ROM.

| Vocabulary words | Known words |
|---|---|
| boil | sink, milk |
| burner | clock, flower |
| candle | boat, glasses |
| container | balloon, truck |
| exhaust | rain, nose |
| liquid | cheese, sandwich |
| melt | snowman, milk |
| plastic | couch, glasses |
| steam | orange, key |
| temperature | toilet, pants |

### Subsequent Presentation

After the initial presentation the pictures of the known words can be put away. The rest of the week, display only the pictures of the vocabulary words and say to children, "Show me _____" (insert vocabulary word) or "What's the word for this?" (point at picture).

# Quick Definitions

**boil**  when water is so hot it bubbles

**burner**  a hot thing that cooks your food on the stove

**candle**  something that you light on fire on your birthday cake

**container**  something that holds stuff

**exhaust**  the cloudy stuff or smoke that comes out of the back of your car

**liquid**  wet stuff like water or juice

**melt**  when ice turns into water

**plastic**  hard stuff that makes up things like LEGOs or soda bottles

**steam**  the smoke that comes out of water when it bubbles

**temperature**  it tells you how hot or cold something is

# CAR Quest

The following are questions that you can ask students about the story you are reading. We suggest reviewing the text beforehand and using sticky notes to mark appropriate places to pause for discussion. The questions are labeled according to the types described in Chapter 3.

## Books

Zoehfeld, K. (1998). *What is the world made of?* New York: HarperCollins.

Garrett, G. (2004). *Solids, liquids, and gases.* Chicago: Children's Press.

Page location describes the picture (illustration or photo) that relates to the individual CAR Quest question. Unknown vocabulary words are *italicized*.

### What Is the World Made Of?

**Page location:** Girl playing with blocks, baby crying in highchair, and boy catching a ball

    **Competence:** What *liquid* has the baby spilled?

    **Relate:** Does anyone see any *liquids* around the room?

    **Abstract:** Would it be good to make a building out of *liquid*?

**Page location:** A pan of water *boiling* on the stove (*burner*)

    **Competence:** Can you point to the *burner* in the picture?

    **Abstract:** What else could you make with a *burner*?

    **Relate:** Have you ever seen a *burner* in real life—maybe in the kitchen?

### Solids, Liquids, and Gases

**Page location:** Icebergs floating in the water

    **Competence:** Can you point to where the ice has *melted*?

    **Abstract:** What are some things you could do to make ice *melt* into a *liquid*?

    **Relate:** Have you ever seen something *melt* in real life? What was it?

**Page location:** Tea kettle on stove

    **Abstract:** What makes the water hot enough to *boil*?

    **Competence:** What made the water *boil* in this picture?

    **Relate:** Have you ever seen your parents *boil* water for cooking?

# Building Bridges—
# Start 'em Up! Topic

I have a bunch of *containers* for things at home. Do you? What do you keep in them? Can they hold *liquids* or just solids?

# New VEhicles—
# Extension Activities

### Activity 1: What Is This Made Of?

**Materials:** Plastic items (e.g., soda bottles, food *containers*, baby toys), *candle*, bowl with water, bowl of ice, paper lunch sacks

**Description:** The paper lunch sacks should be filled with one item (e.g., *plastic* soda bottle, food *container, candle*). One sack should be left empty to demonstrate that it is filled with gas. Blindfold the children and have them place their hands in the lunch sacks or bowls and try to identify what they are touching. Is it a solid, *liquid,* or gas? How do they know? Ask the children the *temperature* of the item they are feeling. Is it hot, cold, or in the middle?

### Activity 2: Solid to Liquid to Gas

**Materials:** Bag of ice, sterno or votive *candle*, matches, bread pan, small frying pan or pot

**Description:** The teacher should place the sterno or votive *candle* on the bottom of the bread pan and light it. Place the frying pan on top of the bread pan rim. Place a small amount of ice in the frying pan. Draw special attention to the *burner* that is heating the pan. Have the children talk about what is happening as the ice *melts* into *liquid* and eventually *boils* to release *steam* (talk about how *steam* is similar to *exhaust*). Talk about the change in *temperature* along the way as well.

# Communication

We provide two types of communication: a classroom posting for students and visitors and a parent letter to be sent home. These are found on the next two pages and on the accompanying CD-ROM.

# Solids, Liquids, and Gases
# Vocabulary Words

boil

burner

candle

container

exhaust

liquid

melt

plastic

steam

temperature

Dear Parents:

This week we will be focusing on vocabulary words for Solids, Liquids, and Gases. We will be reading stories and carrying out activities to help your child learn the meanings of these words. By pointing out examples of these words at home and in the community, you can help your child expand his or her vocabulary. This week's words (with simple definitions that children can understand) are as follows:

| | |
|---|---|
| boil | when water is so hot it bubbles |
| burner | a hot thing that cooks your food on the stove |
| candle | something that you light on fire on your birthday cake |
| container | something that holds stuff |
| exhaust | the cloudy stuff or smoke that comes out of the back of your car |
| liquid | wet stuff like water or juice |
| melt | when ice turns into water |
| plastic | hard stuff that makes up things like LEGOs or soda bottles |
| steam | the smoke that comes out of water when it bubbles |
| temperature | it tells you how hot or cold something is |

Please post this where you and your child can see it. Thanks!

Sincerely,

Your child's teacher

UNIT

**11**

# Trains and Bridges

## Vocabulary

| | |
|---|---|
| arch | locomotive |
| bay | track |
| cable | trestle |
| caboose | tunnel |
| engineer | whistle |

## New VEhicles—
## N3C Vocabulary Introduction

### Initial Presentation

Find pictures for all vocabulary words listed below as well as the two known words paired with each vocabulary word. The known words should be in children's vocabularies. If not, substitute another from the set of pictures that your students are likely to know. In the large-group setting show all three pictures (the vocabulary word and the two known words) randomly to the children and ask them, "Which one is _____?" (insert vocabulary word). The children should be able to infer that the vocabulary word refers to the unknown picture among the three. If you wish, the quick definitions can be introduced then as well. All pictures are included in the accompanying CD-ROM.

| Vocabulary words | Known words |
|---|---|
| arch | bus, door |
| bay | bib, foot |
| cable | baseball, bottle |
| caboose | bike, boat |
| engineer | clown, doctor |
| locomotive | road, horse |
| track | square, run |
| trestle | scissors, house |
| tunnel | triangle, house |
| whistle | bike, phone |

### Subsequent Presentation

After the initial presentation the pictures of the known words can be put away. The rest of the week, display only the pictures of the vocabulary words and say to children, "Show me _____" (insert vocabulary word) or "What's the word for this?" (point at picture).

# Quick Definitions

**arch**   a circle-shaped opening you sometimes see in bridges, tunnels, and doorways

**bay**   a part of the ocean between two pieces of land

**cable**   a thick strong wire used to hold something up

**caboose**   the last car on the train

**engineer**   a person who drives trains

**locomotive**   the front part of the train that pulls it along

**track**   the metal path the train runs on

**trestle**   a bridge for a train

**tunnel**   an underground road

**whistle**   you blow on it to make a loud sound to warn people

# CAR Quest

The following are questions that you can ask students about the story you are reading. We suggest reviewing the text beforehand and using sticky notes to mark appropriate places to pause for discussion. The questions are labeled according to the types described in Chapter 3.

## Books

Neitzel, S. (2000). *I'm taking a trip on my train*. New York: Scholastic.

Hunter, R. (1999). *Cross a bridge*. New York: Scholastic.

Page location describes the picture (illustration or photo) that relates to the individual CAR Quest question. Unknown vocabulary words are *italicized*.

### I'm Taking a Trip on My Train

**Page location:** Picture of striped *engineer* cap

   **Abstract:** Where do you think the *engineer* is going on the train?

   **Competence:** What is the *engineer* wearing?

**Page location:** Picture of *locomotive*

   **Competence:** Where is the *locomotive*?

**Page location:** Picture of *tunnel*

   **Relate:** Have you ever been through a *tunnel*?

**Page location:** Next to the picture of a *tunnel*

   **Abstract:** Why does the train need a *track*?

   **Relate:** Have you ever seen train *tracks*?

### Cross a Bridge

**Page location:** First picture, a bridge over water and a bridge over land

   **Competence:** What kinds of animals live in the *bays*, rivers, and streams?

**Page location:** A river forms natural *arches* through stone.

   **Relate:** Where have you seen an *arch*?

**Page location:** A train crosses a *trestle*.

   **Competence:** What color is the *trestle*?

   **Abstract:** How does the *trestle* help the train get to the other side?

Page location: Bridge over the Arkansas River in Colorado

Relate: Have you ever been on a bridge with *cables*?

Abstract: How do the *cables* help the bridge to stay up?

# Building Bridges—
# Start 'em Up! Topic

Have you ever crossed a bridge or taken a train ride? Tell me all about where you went and what you did there.

# New VEhicles—
# Extension Activities

### Activity 1: Art Activity—Making Trains

Materials: Copy picture of a *locomotive* and *caboose* (provided) for each child, construction paper, scissors, markers/crayons/colored pencils, glue

Description: Have children create their own trains using the materials listed. Have children cut out circles for wheels and rectangles for boxcars. They can cut out the *locomotive* and the *caboose*. A separate sheet of construction paper could be used as a background. Encourage the children to label the different parts of the train (e.g., *locomotive, tracks*). Children should share their work with others at the end of the period.

### Activity 2: Map Drawing—Where Does the Train Go in Our Town?

Materials: Picture of a town (provided), crayons or color pencils

Description: Have children draw their own trains and *tracks* leading to different parts of the town. Have each child talk about his or her work and where his or her train visited.

### Activity 3: Physical Activity—Let's Make a Class Train!

Materials: None

Description: Have children spread out throughout the classroom so that they cannot touch one another with hands outstretched. Select one child as the *locomotive* and another as the *caboose*. The *locomotive* will pretend to blow a *whistle* ("Toot! Toot!") and start walking near other children, picking them up along the way (the children should place their hands onto the moving child's shoulders). This should continue until the *caboose* is picked up last, possibly ending in one complete loop around the room. The children can pretend to go over a bridge held up by a *cable* across the *bay*, under the *arch*, through a *tunnel*, over a *trestle*, and so forth. The teacher (or lead child) can talk about where they are going using the vocabulary. The activity can be repeated using others as the *locomotive* and *caboose*.

# Communication

We provide two types of communication: a classroom posting for students and visitors and a parent letter to be sent home. These are found on the next two pages and on the accompanying CD-ROM.

Dear Parents,

This week we will be focusing on vocabulary words for Trains and Bridges. We will be reading stories and carrying out activities to help your child learn the meanings of these words. By pointing out examples of these words at home and in the community, you can help your child expand his or her vocabulary. This week's words (with simple definitions that children can understand) are as follows:

| | |
|---|---|
| arch | a circle-shaped opening you sometimes see in bridges, tunnels, and doorways |
| bay | a part of the ocean between two pieces of land |
| cable | a thick strong wire used to hold something up |
| caboose | the last car on the train |
| engineer | a person who drives trains |
| locomotive | the front part of the train that pulls it along |
| track | the metal path the train runs on |
| trestle | a bridge for a train |
| tunnel | an underground road |
| whistle | you blow on it to make a loud sound to warn people |

Please post this where you and your child can see it. Thanks!

Sincerely,

Your child's teacher

UNIT

12
# Transportation

## Vocabulary

| | |
|---|---|
| cargo | sailboat |
| helicopter | scooter |
| motor | submarine |
| oar | taxi |
| pedal | tire |

## New VEhicles—
## N3C Vocabulary Introduction

### Initial Presentation

Find pictures for all vocabulary words listed below as well as the two known words paired with each vocabulary word. The known words should be in children's vocabularies. If not, substitute another from the set of pictures that your students are likely to know. In the large-group setting show all three pictures (the vocabulary word and the two known words) randomly to the children and ask them, "Which one is _____?" (insert vocabulary word). The children should be able to infer that the vocabulary word refers to the unknown picture among the three. If you wish, the quick definitions can be introduced then as well. All pictures are included in the accompanying CD-ROM.

| Vocabulary words | Known words |
|---|---|
| cargo | book, circle |
| helicopter | bike, truck |
| motor | train, swing |
| oar | carrot, saw |
| pedal | sock, hand |
| sailboat | swing, plane |
| scooter | orange, jump |
| submarine | sink, hammer |
| taxi | bed, train |
| tire | apple, TV |

### Subsequent Presentation

After the initial presentation the pictures of the known words can be put away. The rest of the week, display only the pictures of the vocabulary words and say to children, "Show me _____" (insert vocabulary word) or "What's the word for this?" (point at picture).

# Quick Definitions

**cargo**   things that are carried by a ship or an airplane

**helicopter**   a flying machine with long blades that spin around on top

**motor**   a machine that makes things go

**oar**   a flat piece of wood you use to steer boats

**pedal**   a part of a bicycle, car, or piano that you push with your foot

**sailboat**   a boat that uses the wind to move with

**scooter**   something you ride on that has two wheels and a tall handle

**submarine**   a boat that goes under the water

**taxi**   a car whose driver you pay to take you somewhere

**tire**   wheels on a car, truck, or bicycle

# CAR Quest

The following are questions that you can ask students about the story you are reading. We suggest reviewing the text beforehand and using sticky notes to mark appropriate places to pause for discussion. The questions are labeled according to the types described in Chapter 3.

## Books

Morris, A. (1990). *On the go*. New York: Scholastic.

Ziefert, H. (2005). *From Kalamazoo to Timbuktu*. Maplewood, NJ: Blue Apple Books.

Page location describes the picture (illustration or photo) that relates to the individual CAR Quest question. Unknown vocabulary words are *italicized*.

### On the Go

**Page location:** Busy city scene with people riding bicycles

**Competence:** Where are the *pedals* on this?

**Relate:** When have you used *pedals*? What sort of things have you *pedaled*?

**Page location:** A red car next to a double decker bus

**Abstract:** What do you think the *motor* does?

**Competence:** Which items on this page have a *motor*?

**Page location:** Plane with baggage carriers

**Competence:** Where do you see the *cargo* on this page?

**Abstract:** Where do you think the *cargo* is going next?

**Page location:** *Helicopter* lifting off

**Relate:** Has anyone seen a *helicopter* before? What does it look like? Would you ever want to take a ride in a *helicopter*?

### From Kalamazoo to Timbuktu

**Page location:** A *helicopter* flies above the town.

**Abstract:** Why did Millie take out her red bandana when the bus blew its *tires*?

**Relate:** Have you ever been on a bus or in a car when a *tire* popped? What happened?

**Page location:** Mike and Millie paddle a boat while fish, dolphins, and a sea turtle swim below.

    **Relate:** Would you want to use an *oar* to get all the way across the ocean?

    **Abstract:** Do you think it would be easier for them to use a *sailboat*?

**Page location:** Mike and Millie in a *sailboat*

    **Competence:** What are those animals flying around the *sailboat*?

    **Competence:** What animals are swimming around the *sailboat*?

# Building Bridges— Start 'em Up! Topic

If you could go on a *helicopter, sailboat, taxi, submarine,* or *scooter,* which would you choose? Where would you go?

# New VEhicles— Extension Activities

## Activity 1: Sorting Transportation by Characteristics

**Materials:** Picture cards of types of transportation (e.g., *helicopter, scooter, submarine, taxi*), picture cards of words associated with different types of transportation (e.g., *carries cargo,* has *pedals,* has *motors,* has *oars*)

**Description:** The purpose of the activity is to have children practice discussing the attributes of various modes of transportation and sorting by the presence or absence of that attribute. Have children sort the transportation pictures by each classification (e.g., Does it carry *cargo*? Does it have *pedals*? Does it have *tires*?). Have children carry this out in pairs or as a group. They should talk together about what they are doing and why they are doing it. Repeat a number of times using each of the sorting classifications. If there is time, children can offer their own ideas of attributes by which they could sort the transportation (e.g., has seats, has windows, goes fast, goes slow).

## Activity 2: How Would You Get There from Here?

**Materials:** Transportation pictures from Activity 1

**Description:** Talk with children about the kinds of transportation they have used to get from one place to another and about the kinds of transportation they have seen in their communities. Show students the picture cards for transportation. Have each child take turns thinking of a destination to which he or she would like to go. Explain to the children that you will be looking at the different ways that we get from one place to another. Make sure they understand that different children in the group might use different modes of transportation to get from one place to another. Place the pictures of modes of transportation within reach so that children can use them if they need to refer to them. Have the children discuss the travel destination offered by the child and whether they would like to go there, too. Have them discuss how they might get from here to the destination. Some destinations might require multiple modes of transportation, so encourage the children to consider all of the different types of transportation they might use.

# Communication

We provide two types of communication: a classroom posting for students and visitors and a parent letter to be sent home. These can be found on the next two pages and on the accompanying CD-ROM.

# Transportation Vocabulary Words

cargo

helicopter

motor

oar

pedal

sailboat

scooter

submarine

taxi

tire

Dear Parents,

This week we will be focusing on vocabulary words for Transportation. We will be reading stories and carrying out activities to help your child learn the meanings of these words. By pointing out examples of these words at home and in the community, you can help your child expand his or her vocabulary. This week's words (with simple definitions that children can understand) are as follows:

| | |
|---|---|
| cargo | things that are carried by a ship or an airplane |
| helicopter | a flying machine with long blades that spin around on top |
| motor | a machine that makes things go |
| oar | a flat piece of wood you use to steer boats |
| pedal | a part of a bicycle, car, or piano that you push with your foot |
| sailboat | a boat that uses the wind to move with |
| scooter | something you ride on that has two wheels and a tall handle |
| submarine | a boat that goes under the water |
| taxi | a car whose driver you pay to take you somewhere |
| tire | wheel on a car, truck, or bicycle |

Please post this where you and your child can see it. Thanks!

Sincerely,

Your child's teacher

UNIT
13
# Hooray for School!

- - - - - - - - - - - - - - - - - - - - - - - - - - - - - - - - - - - - - - - - - -

## Vocabulary

| | |
|---|---|
| backpack | eraser |
| cafeteria | gymnasium |
| calendar | hall |
| centers | lunchbox |
| desk | supplies |

## New VEhicles— N3C Vocabulary Introduction

### Initial Presentation

Find pictures for all vocabulary words listed below as well as the two known words paired with each vocabulary word. The known words should be in children's vocabularies. If not, substitute another from the set of pictures that your students are likely to know. In the large-group setting, show all three pictures (the vocabulary word and the two known words) randomly to the children and ask them, "Which one is _____?" (insert vocabulary word). The children should be able to infer that the vocabulary word refers to the unknown picture among the three. If you wish, the quick definitions can be introduced then as well. All pictures are included in the accompanying CD-ROM.

| Vocabulary words | Known words |
|---|---|
| backpack | baseball, foot |
| cafeteria | box, door |
| calendar | clock, crayon |
| centers | boat, traffic light |
| desk | bat, bed |
| eraser | ball, hotdog |
| gymnasium | shoe, hand |
| hall | chair, table |
| lunchbox | bag, bottle |
| supplies | teacher, piano |

### Subsequent Presentation

After the initial presentation the pictures of the known words can be put away. The rest of the week, display only the pictures of the vocabulary words and say to children, "Show me _____" (insert vocabulary word) or "What's the word for this?" (point at picture).

## Quick Definitions

**backpack**   a bag you use to carry things you need for school

**cafeteria**   a room in your school where you can go and eat

**calendar**   a chart that shows the days, weeks, and months of the year

**centers**   places in the classroom where you play things like housekeeping, do art, or read books

**desk**   what your teacher sits at to write or draw

**eraser**   the pink thing on the end of your pencil

**gymnasium**   a big room at school where you can run and play ball

**hall**   a place you walk between classrooms at school

**lunchbox**   what you carry your lunch in

**supplies**   all the stuff that you need for school

## CAR Quest

The following are questions that you can ask students about the story you are reading. We suggest reviewing the text beforehand and using sticky notes to mark appropriate places to pause for discussion. The questions are labeled according to the types described in Chapter 3.

### Books

Rockwell, A. (2001). *Welcome to kindergarten.* New York: Walker & Company.

Wing, N. (2005). *The night before kindergarten.* New York: Grosset & Dunlap.

Page location describes the picture (illustration or photo) that relates to the individual CAR Quest question. Unknown vocabulary words are *italicized.*

#### Welcome to Kindergarten

**Page location:** A girl with red hair and pink pants shows the mother and son where to go.

**Competence:** Can you point to the *hall* in the picture?

**Abstract:** Where do you think the *hall* leads to?

**Page location:** The boy in the striped shirt looks at a cup of soil and some seeds.

**Competence:** What things do you see in the science *center*?

**Relate:** What kinds of things would you want to learn about in a science *center*?

**Page location:** Picture of a *calendar*

**Abstract:** What do the numbers on the *calendar* tell us?

**Relate:** Do you have a *calendar* at home? Where is it?

#### The Night Before Kindergarten

**Page location:** Two children who are sleeping dream about school *supplies.*

**Relate:** Did you bring any school *supplies* with you today? What did you bring?

**Abstract:** What does it mean to have school *supplies* dance in your head?

**Page location:** We can see in the windows of the house at nighttime.

    **Relate:** Have you ever used an *eraser* before?

    **Abstract:** Why do you need to bring an *eraser* to school with you?

    **Competence:** Where are the *backpacks*?

**Page location:** The teacher greets the parents and children.

    **Competence:** Can you show me who is carrying a *lunchbox*?

# Building Bridges—
# Start 'em Up! Topics

What did you and your parents do to help you get ready for school today?

# New VEhicles—
# Extension Activities

## Activity 1: My First Day of School

**Materials:** Paper, tape, crayons/markers/pencils

**Description:** Have students draw a picture about their first day in school. Have students decorate labels to place on their school *supplies*.

## Activity 2: School Supply List for Parents

**Materials:** Paper, crayons/markers/pencils

**Description:** Read through a *supply* list and have children draw pictures of the associated *supplies* (e.g., *backpack, eraser, lunchbox*). Have the children take that list and their drawings with their parents when purchasing *supplies* (e.g., crayon, *eraser*, glue).

## Activity 3: Classroom Labels

**Materials:** Paper, tape, crayons/markers/pencils

**Description:** Have students decorate a name tag that can be placed on their cubbies or storage areas for their *backpacks*. Have students help create the signs for the *centers* in the classroom (arithmetic *center*, writing workshop, computer *center*). Templates for creating labels can be found at http://www.abcteach.com/free/l/labels_school_set.pdf

# Communication

We provide two types of communication: a classroom posting for students and visitors and a parent letter to be sent home. These are found on the next two pages and on the accompanying CD-ROM.

# Hooray for School!
# Vocabulary Words

backpack

cafeteria

calendar

centers

desk

eraser

gymnasium

hall

lunchbox

supplies

Dear Parents,

This week we will be focusing on vocabulary words for Hooray for School! We will be reading stories and carrying out activities to help your child learn the meanings of these words. By pointing out examples of these words at home and in the community, you can help your child expand his or her vocabulary. This week's words (with simple definitions that children can understand) are as follows:

| | |
|---|---|
| backpack | a bag you use to carry things you need for school |
| cafeteria | a room in your school where you can go and eat |
| calendar | a chart that shows the days, weeks, and months of the year |
| centers | places in the classroom where you play things like housekeeping, do art, or read books |
| desk | what your teacher sits at to write or draw |
| eraser | the pink thing on the end of your pencil |
| gymnasium | a big room at school where you can run and play ball |
| hall | a place you walk between classrooms at school |
| lunchbox | what you carry your lunch in |
| supplies | all the stuff that you need for school |

Please post this where you and your child can see it. Thanks!

Sincerely,

Your child's teacher

UNIT

**14**

# Careers and Community Helpers

## Vocabulary

| | |
|---|---|
| architect | crossing guard |
| artist | judge |
| athlete | nurse |
| baker | police officer |
| carpenter | veterinarian |

## New VEhicles—
## N3C Vocabulary Introduction

### Initial Presentation

Find pictures for all vocabulary words listed below as well as the two known words paired with each vocabulary word. The known words should be in children's vocabularies. If not, substitute another from the set of pictures that your students are likely to know. In the large-group setting show all three pictures (the vocabulary word and the two known words) randomly to the children and ask them, "Which one is _____?" (insert vocabulary word). The children should be able to infer that the vocabulary word refers to the unknown picture among the three. If you wish, the quick definitions can be introduced then as well. All pictures are included in the accompanying CD-ROM.

| Vocabulary words | Known words |
|---|---|
| architect | sink, pants |
| artist | clown, crayon |
| athlete | slide, foot |
| baker | boat, swing |
| carpenter | stick, crayon |
| crossing guard | traffic light, fireman |
| judge | policeman, fireman |
| nurse | coat, nose |
| police officer | traffic light, baseball |
| veterinarian | teacher, table |

### Subsequent Presentation

After the initial presentation the pictures of the known words can be put away. The rest of the week, display only the pictures of the vocabulary words and say to children, "Show me _____" (insert vocabulary word) or "What's the word for this?" (point at picture).

# Quick Definitions

**architect**   someone who plans how to build things

**artist**   someone who draws pictures

**athlete**   someone who knows how to do a sport such as football well

**baker**   someone who cooks cookies, cake, and bread

**carpenter**   someone who builds things with wood

**crossing guard**   someone who helps you across the street

**judge**   someone who decides how someone should be punished for doing
   something wrong

**nurse**   someone who helps doctors take care of sick people

**police officer**   someone who keeps us safe from bad people

**veterinarian**   someone who takes care of sick animals

# CAR Quest

The following are questions that you can ask students about the story you are reading. We suggest reviewing the text beforehand and using sticky notes to mark appropriate places to pause for discussion. The questions are labeled according to the types described in Chapter 3.

## Books

Rockwell, A. (2001). *Career day.* New York: Scholastic.

Louise, T. (2007). *When I grow up.* New York: Abrams Books for Young Readers.

Page location describes the picture (illustration or photo) that relates to the individual CAR Quest question. Unknown vocabulary words are *italicized.*

### Career Day

**Page location:** Picture of a *judge* in the courtroom

> **Competence:** What is the *judge* wearing?

> **Abstract:** She is pounding her gavel and saying, "Order in the court!" Why does the *judge* need order?

> **Relate:** Would you want to be a *judge* when you grow up?

**Page location:** The *crossing guard* helps children cross the street.

> **Competence:** What is the *crossing guard* wearing?

> **Relate:** Have you ever seen a *crossing guard* outside your school?

**Page location:** A *veterinarian* examines a dog.

> **Abstract:** Why is the *veterinarian* looking at the dog?

### When I Grow Up

**Page location:** City buildings

> **Abstract:** What do you think the *architect* uses in his or her job?

> **Relate:** What kinds of things would you build if you were an *architect*?

**Page location:** Girl thinks about being a *nurse*

    **Abstract:** What might a *nurse* do to take care of someone?

    **Relate:** Would you want to be a *nurse* and take care of sick people?

**Page location:** Picture of a *police officer*

    **Competence:** Where is the *police officer* doing his job?

**Page location:** Picture of an *athlete*

    **Competence:** What is the *athlete* doing?

# Building Bridges—
# Start 'em Up! Topic

What career would you like to have when you grow up? Why?

# New VEhicles—
# Extension Activities

### Activity 1: Matching the Profession with the Instruments Game

**Materials:** Unit pictures for *nurse, veterinarian, carpenter, crossing guard, judge, architect, artist, athlete, baker;* downloaded Google Images for stethoscope, dog, hammer, house, stop sign, gavel, paintbrush, football, cake

**Description:** Have children match the pictures of the instruments to the target word pictures to which they belong (e.g., *nurse* to stethoscope).

### Activity 2: Let's Choose a Career!

**Materials:** Target word pictures included with the unit plus the pictures for teacher, doctor, dentist, clown, and fireman.

**Description:** Ask children to pick the picture of the career they would like to have. Ask them to discuss what they like and don't like about various careers. Let them explain to other children in the group why they chose that career.

### Activity 3: Let's Pretend!

**Materials:** Clothing items and/or props related to the careers: scrubs, stethoscope, nurse's hat, goggles, apron, paint brushes, microscope, graduation robes, paper, gavel, calculator, pencils, shovel, magnifying glass, badge, tools, football, broken computer

**Description:** Have children pretend to have various careers.

# Communication

We provide two types of communication: a classroom posting for students and visitors and a parent letter to be sent home. These are found on the next two pages and on the accompanying CD-ROM.

# Careers and Community Helpers Vocabulary Words

architect

artist

athlete

baker

carpenter

crossing guard

judge

nurse

police officer

veterinarian

Dear Parents,

This week we will be focusing on vocabulary words for Careers and Community Helpers. We will be reading stories and carrying out activities to help your child learn the meanings of these words. By pointing out examples of these words at home and in the community, you can help your child expand his or her vocabulary. This week's words (with simple definitions that children can understand) are as follows:

| | |
|---|---|
| **architect** | someone who plans how to build things |
| **artist** | someone who draws pictures |
| **athlete** | someone who knows how to do a sport such as football well |
| **baker** | someone who cooks cookies, cake, and bread |
| **carpenter** | someone who builds things with wood |
| **crossing guard** | someone who helps you across the street |
| **judge** | someone who decides how someone should be punished for doing something wrong |
| **nurse** | someone who helps doctors take care of sick people |
| **police officer** | someone who keeps us safe from bad people |
| **veterinarian** | someone who takes care of sick animals |

Please post this where you and your child can see it. Thanks!

Sincerely,

Your child's teacher

# Fire Safety

---

## Vocabulary

| | |
|---|---|
| battery | mask |
| flames | nozzle |
| helmet | pickax |
| hose | siren |
| hydrant | smoke |

## New VEhicles—
## N3C Vocabulary Introduction

### Initial Presentation

Find pictures for all vocabulary words listed below as well as the two known words paired with each vocabulary word. The known words should be in children's vocabularies. If not, substitute another from the set of pictures that your students are likely to know. In the large-group setting, show all three pictures (the vocabulary word and the two known words) randomly to the children and ask them, "Which one is _____?" (insert vocabulary word). The children should be able to infer that the vocabulary word refers to the unknown picture among the three. If you wish, the quick definitions can be introduced then as well. All pictures are included in the accompanying CD-ROM.

| Vocabulary words | Known words |
|---|---|
| battery | bus, crayon |
| flames | bell, fork |
| helmet | bag, book |
| hose | sock, eye |
| hydrant | circle, fridge |
| mask | boot, eye |
| nozzle | balloon, saw |
| pickax | bat, shirt |
| siren | TV, train |
| smoke | fireman, hat |

### Subsequent Presentation

After the initial presentation the pictures of the known words can be put away. The rest of the week, display only the pictures of the vocabulary words and say to children, "Show me _____" (insert vocabulary word) or "What's the word for this?" (point at picture).

# Quick Definitions

**battery**  it makes flashlights and cell phones work

**flames**  the part of fire that is bright and moves around

**helmet**  a hat you wear on your head to protect it

**hose**  a long round tube for spraying water

**hydrant**  it is on the street and is where the fireman gets his water

**mask**  something you wear to protect your face

**nozzle**  it goes on the end of a hose to point water at something

**pickax**  something you use to chop something down

**siren**  it makes a loud warning sound on a fire engine, police car, or ambulance

**smoke**  it makes the air all gray when something is burning

# CAR Quest

The following are questions that you can ask students about the story you are reading. We suggest reviewing the text beforehand and using sticky notes to mark appropriate places to pause for discussion. The questions are labeled according to the types described in Chapter 3.

## Books

Bridwell, N. (2005). *Clifford the firehouse dog*. New York: Scholastic.

Demarest, C.L. (2001). *Firefighters A to Z*. New York: Scholastic.

Page location describes the picture (illustration or photo) that relates to the individual CAR Quest question. Unknown vocabulary words are *italicized*.

### Clifford the Firehouse Dog

**Page location:** Nero points to the Fire Safety poster of a person on fire (look at the *flames*).

> **Abstract:** How do you think *flames* could get on your clothes?

> **Abstract:** Why is it important for the children to learn how to put *flames* out if their clothes catch fire?

**Page location:** Emily Elizabeth pays the man with the broken vegetable cart and they hear a *siren*.

> **Relate:** Have you ever heard the *siren* on a fire engine?

**Page location:** Nero helps unroll the *hose*.

> **Competence:** What is Clifford doing to the *hose*?

**Page location:** Nero blows the *smoke* out of the building.

> **Competence:** Where is the *smoke*?

**Page location:** Clifford reviews the fire safety rule, last page.

> **Relate:** Do you have a *battery* in any of your toys?

### Firefighters A to Z

**Page location:** Letter C

> **Relate:** This firefighter is wearing a *helmet*. Have you ever seen anyone else wear a *helmet*?

> **Abstract:** Why would you want to wear a *helmet* around a fire?

Page location: Letter H

Competence: What color is the *hydrant*?

Page location: Letter M

Relate: Have you ever worn a different kind of *mask* on Halloween?

Page location: Letter N

Abstract: What is the firefighter thinking about when he is pointing the *nozzle* of his *hose*?

Page location: Letter P

Competence: What is the firefighter doing with his *pickax*?

# Building Bridges—
# Start 'em Up! Topic

Where were you the last time you saw a fire engine?

# New VEhicles—
# Extension Activities

## Activity 1: Let's Be a Firefighter

**Materials:** Plastic tubing (for *hose*), inexpensive firefighter *helmet*

**Description:** Have some children pretend to be firefighters and others pretend to be people rescued by the firefighters. Have the children being rescued crawl on the ground to get down below the *smoke*. Do the firefighters need to wear *masks*? Should they bring a *pickax*? What else do they need?

## Activity 2: Making Smoke Detectors

**Materials:** Two small paper plates (or children can cut out circles from construction paper), one small rectangle (for a *battery*), Check Your Smoke Detector Batteries label (supplied), red marker, tape, scissors

**Description:** Have children tape the *battery* to one side of the plate. Have the children staple or tape the two plates (or circles) together and decorate them with a red dot and the Check Your Smoke Detector Batteries label. Ask the children to notice the *smoke* detectors in their classroom and homes. The take-home product is a good reminder for parents to install detectors and to check those *batteries*!

## Activity 3: Practicing "Stop, Drop, and Roll"

**Materials:** Orange and yellow sticky notes, picture of *flames*

**Description:** Have children cut out orange and yellow sticky notes in the shape of *flames* using the picture of *flames* as a guide. Have the children take turns pretending to hear the *smoke* alarm and sticking the *flames* on one another's clothes. One child says, "I smell *smoke*. I see *flames*. Stop, drop, and roll!" until the *flames* fall off the clothes.

### Activity 4: I'm a Firefighter

**Materials:** Vocabulary pictures for *helmet, mask, siren, smoke, pickax, hose, nozzle, flames*

**Description:** Everyone gets a vocabulary picture from the song. Sing the following song to the tune of *Here We Go 'Round the Mulberry Bush* and have each child hold up his or her picture at the proper stanza.

This is the way I wear my *helmet*, wear my *helmet*, wear my *helmet*.

This is the way I wear my *helmet*. I'm a firefighter.

This is the way I wear my *mask*, wear my *mask*, wear my *mask*.

This is the way I wear my *mask*. I'm a firefighter.

This is the noise the *siren* makes (wheer!), *siren* makes, *siren* makes.

This is the noise the *siren* makes. I'm a firefighter.

This is the way I smell the *smoke* (sniff, sniff), smell the *smoke*, smell the *smoke*.

This is the way I smell the *smoke*. I'm a firefighter.

This is the way I use my *pickax*, use my *pickax*, use my *pickax*.

This is the way I use my *pickax*. I'm a firefighter.

This is the way I fasten the *nozzle*, fasten the *nozzle*, fasten the *nozzle*.

This is the way I fasten the *nozzle*. I'm a firefighter.

This is the way I point the *hose*, point the *hose*, point the *hose*.

This is the way I point the *hose*. I'm a firefighter.

This is the way we put out the *flames*, put out the *flames*, put out the *flames*.

This is the way we put out the *flames*. I'm a firefighter.

## Communication

We provide two types of communication: a classroom posting for students and visitors and a parent letter to be sent home. These are on the next two pages and on the accompanying CD-ROM.

# Fire Safety Vocabulary Words

battery

flames

helmet

hose

hydrant

mask

nozzle

pickax

siren

smoke

Dear Parents:

This week we will be focusing on vocabulary words for Fire Safety. We will be reading stories and carrying out activities to help your child learn the meanings of these words. By pointing out examples of these words at home and in the community, you can help your child expand his or her vocabulary. This week's words (with simple definitions that children can understand) are as follows:

| | |
|---|---|
| battery | it makes flashlights and cell phones work |
| flames | the part of fire that is bright and moves around |
| helmet | a hat you wear on your head to protect it |
| hose | a long round tube for spraying water |
| hydrant | it is on the street and is where the fireman gets his water |
| mask | something you wear to protect your face |
| nozzle | it goes on the end of a hose to point water at something |
| pickax | something you use to chop something down |
| siren | it makes a loud warning sound on a fire engine, police car, or ambulance |
| smoke | it makes the air all gray when something is burning |

Please post this where you and your child can see it. Thanks!

Sincerely,

Your child's teacher

# Food Preparation

## Vocabulary

| | |
|---|---|
| cinnamon | plantation |
| flour | recipe |
| ingredients | sieve |
| measuring cup | spatula |
| orchard | wheat |

## New VEhicles—
## N3C Vocabulary Introduction

### Initial Presentation

Find pictures for all vocabulary words listed below as well as the two known words paired with each vocabulary word. The known words should be in children's vocabularies. If not, substitute another from the set of pictures that your students are likely to know. In the large-group setting, show all three pictures (the vocabulary word and the two known words) randomly to the children and ask them, "Which one is _____?" (insert vocabulary word). The children should be able to infer that the vocabulary word refers to the unknown picture among the three. If you wish, the quick definitions can be introduced then as well. All pictures are included in the accompanying CD-ROM.

| Vocabulary words | Known words |
|---|---|
| cinnamon | bat, bread |
| flour | cookie, fork |
| ingredients | cake, fridge |
| measuring cup | toothbrush, milk |
| orchard | couch, hamburger |
| plantation | pumpkin, king |
| recipe | orange, mouth |
| sieve | stove, hamburger |
| spatula | cheese, phone |
| wheat | apple, stove |

### Subsequent Presentation

After the initial presentation the pictures of the known words can be put away. The rest of the week, display only the pictures of the vocabulary words and say to children, "Show me _____" (insert vocabulary word) or "What's the word for this?" (point at picture).

## Quick Definitions

**cinnamon**  a kind of flavor that smells and tastes very nice; it's the brown stuff in coffee cake

**flour**  wheat that's all ground up; you make cookies and cakes out of it

**ingredients**  stuff that you mix up with other things to make something, like a cake

**measuring cup**  a cup you use to tell how much there is of something

**orchard**  a farm where fruit grows on trees

**plantation**  a farm in a hot place

**recipe**  directions for making food

**sieve**  something you use to sort the big things from the little things

**spatula**  something flat you use in cooking, like for flipping hamburgers or spreading frosting

**wheat**  a plant you make bread from

## CAR Quest

The following are questions that you can ask students about the story you are reading. We suggest reviewing the text beforehand and using sticky notes to mark appropriate places to pause for discussion. The questions are labeled according to the types described in Chapter 3.

### Books

Priceman, M. (1994). *How to make an apple pie and see the world.* New York: Alfred A. Knopf.

Christelow, E. (2004). *Five little monkeys bake a birthday cake.* New York: Houghton Mifflin.

Page location describes the picture (illustration or photo) that relates to the individual CAR Quest question. Unknown vocabulary words are *italicized*.

### *How to Make an Apple Pie and See the World*

**Page location:** First picture, girl reading list of *ingredients*

> **Relate:** Have you ever cooked anything? Did you have all the *ingredients* you needed?

**Page location:** Gathering *wheat* into haystacks

> **Competence:** Where is the *wheat* in the picture?

**Page location:** Girl shakes hand with a cow, cows grazing in the background

> **Abstract:** Why do you think she needs to fill up her *measuring cup* with milk?

**Page location:** Jamaican children dancing in the field, girl overhead in plane

> **Competence:** Who is flying with the girl over the *plantation*?

> **Abstract:** How is this *plantation* different than a garden?

**Page location:** Girl on ladder picking apples in the *orchard*

> **Relate:** Have you ever seen fruit growing in an *orchard*? Where was it?

### *Five Little Monkeys Bake a Birthday Cake*

**Page location:** Monkeys gather around a bowl talking about how much they need of each *ingredient*.

> **Abstract:** Why does the monkey want to read the *recipe*?

> **Relate:** Has you mother ever used a *recipe*? When?

**Page location:** Two monkeys hold their nose, two sift, and one reads the *recipe* book.

> **Competence:** Can you point to the *sieve* they are using to sift?

> **Abstract:** Why would the sifted *flour* make you sneeze?

**Page location:** Two monkeys sneeze as *flour* flies through the air.

> **Competence:** What is happening with the *flour*?

**Page location:** Two firefighters and the monkeys frost the cake.

> **Relate:** They are all using *spatulas* to put the frosting on the cake. Have you ever frosted a cake with a *spatula*?

# Building Bridges—
# Start 'em Up! Topic

What is your favorite food? Why do you like it so much?

# New VEhicles—
# Extension Activities

## Activity 1: Following a Recipe for Playdough

**Materials:** Mixing bowl, *measuring cup, spatula, sieve, flour,* salt, water, small plastic bag

**Description:** Write the following *recipe* up on the board and point out the features, products, *ingredients,* and directions. (You can substitute any recipe in which *spatulas, sieves,* and/or *measuring cups* are used.)

> Easy Playdough
> - 1 cup *flour*
> - 1 cup salt
> - 1 cup water

Have one child measure 1 cup of *flour* with a *measuring cup.* Have another sift the *flour* through a *sieve* into a bowl. Have another measure 1 cup of salt and add to the *flour.* Have another mix with a *spatula.* Have another measure 1 cup of water and gradually add it to the *flour*/salt mixture until it has the consistency of playdough. Have the children take turns kneading the dough. Have them each take some home in a plastic bag.

## Activity 2: Making Recipes

**Materials:** Paper, pictures of vocabulary words (provided), pencils, markers, colored pencils

**Description:** Students will divide a sheet of paper into three columns. In the first they will draw the *ingredients* for their *recipe,* in the second they will include cooking tools, and in the third they will list the source of their ingredients. Children will create their own *recipes* and share their products with the other children.

# Communication

We provide two types of communication: a classroom posting for students and visitors and a parent letter to be sent home. These are on the next two pages and on the accompanying CD-ROM.

# Food Preparation
# Vocabulary Words

cinnamon

flour

ingredients

measuring cup

orchard

plantation

recipe

sieve

spatula

wheat

Dear Parents:

This week we will be focusing on vocabulary words for Food Preparation. We will be reading stories and carrying out activities to help your child learn the meanings of these words. By pointing out examples of these words at home and in the community, you can help your child expand his or her vocabulary. This week's words (with simple definitions that children can understand) are as follows:

| | |
|---|---|
| cinnamon | a kind of flavor that smells and tastes very nice; it's the brown stuff in coffee cake |
| flour | wheat that's all ground up; you make cookies and cakes out of it |
| ingredients | stuff that you mix up with other things to make something, like a cake |
| measuring cup | a cup you use to tell how much there is of something |
| orchard | a farm where fruit grows on trees |
| plantation | a farm in a hot place |
| recipe | directions for making food |
| sieve | something you use to sort the big things from the little things |
| spatula | something flat you use in cooking, like for flipping hamburgers or spreading frosting |
| wheat | a plant you make bread from |

Please post this where you and your child can see it. Thanks!

Sincerely,

Your child's teacher

UNIT
**17**
# Landforms

## Vocabulary

| | |
|---|---|
| boulder | gravel |
| canyon | lake |
| cliff | ocean |
| delta | trench |
| desert | volcano |

## New VEhicles—
## N3C Vocabulary Introduction

### Initial Presentation

Find pictures for all vocabulary words listed below as well as the two known words paired with each vocabulary word. The known words should be in children's vocabularies. If not, substitute another from the set of pictures that your students are likely to know. In the large-group setting show all three pictures (the vocabulary word and the two known words) randomly to the children and ask them, "Which one is _____?" (insert vocabulary word). The children should be able to infer that the vocabulary word refers to the unknown picture among the three. If you wish, the quick definitions can be introduced then as well. All pictures are included in the accompanying CD-ROM.

| Vocabulary words | Known words |
|---|---|
| boulder | baseball, hotdog |
| canyon | bridge, door |
| cliff | hat, flower |
| delta | boat, cup |
| desert | shoe, dress |
| gravel | stairs, hammer |
| lake | tree, horse |
| ocean | cup, milk |
| trench | sink, mouth |
| volcano | sun, drum |

### Subsequent Presentation

After the initial presentation the pictures of the known words can be put away. The rest of the week, display only the pictures of the vocabulary words and say to children, "Show me _____" (insert vocabulary word) or "What's the word for this?" (point at picture).

# Quick Definitions

**boulder**    a large, round rock

**canyon**    the part of the river with high sides reaching to the sky

**cliff**    the edge of a high mountain

**delta**    where a river connects to the sea

**desert**    a dry place where it doesn't rain a lot

**gravel**    small, loose stones or rocks used for paths and roads

**lake**    water surrounded by land

**ocean**    salty water that covers most of the earth

**trench**    a long, skinny hole in the ground

**volcano**    a mountain that spits out very hot liquid

# CAR Quest

The following are questions that you can ask students about the story you are reading. We suggest reviewing the text beforehand and using sticky notes to mark appropriate places to pause for discussion. The questions are labeled according to the types described in Chapter 3.

## Books

Fowler, A. (1995). *The earth is mostly ocean*. New York: Scholastic

Bauer, M. (2006). *Wonders of America: The Grand Canyon*. New York: Aladdin Paperbacks.

Page location describes the picture (illustration or photo) that relates to the individual CAR Quest question. Unknown vocabulary words are *italicized*.

### The Earth Is Mostly Ocean

Page location: Two polar bears on ice

   **Abstract:** What other kinds of animals live near the Arctic *Ocean*?

   **Abstract:** Do you think the Arctic *Ocean* would be cold, warm, or hot?

Page location: Two boys playing on the beach

   **Relate:** Have any of you accidentally swallowed some *ocean* water at the beach? What did it taste like?

   **Competence:** Can anyone point to the *ocean*?

Page location: Illustration of Mt. Everest and the the Mariana *Trench*

   **Relate:** What is about seven miles from here? Can you imagine how deep that *trench* must be?

   **Competence:** Is this *trench* on land or in water?

### Wonders of America: The Grand Canyon

Page location: First illustration

   **Relate:** Has anyone ever visited the Grand *Canyon*?

   **Competence:** What is in the bottom of the *canyon*?

**Page location:** Picture with arrows showing the movement of *boulders* and *gravel* in the river current

**Abstract:** Is the *gravel* larger or smaller than a grain of sand?

**Relate:** Have you ever played with *gravel* outside?

**Competence:** What shape are the *boulders* in this picture?

**Abstract:** Do you think it would be easier to pick up some *gravel* or a *boulder*? Why?

# Building Bridges—
# Start 'em Up! Topic

What kinds of landforms are there around where you live?

# New VEhicles—
# Extension Activities

### Activity 1: Making Landform Shapes with Playdough or Clay

**Materials:** Playdough or clay, whichever is available (see the Food Preparation unit for recipe)

**Description:** Children will be shown how to make a *volcano* (tear off the top of the pyramid and use the material to make lava running down the side), a *boulder* (ball together), a *canyon* (fold together to make a U-shape), and *trench* (extend the U-shape down to make it skinny). Ask children what other kinds of landforms they can make using the clay or playdough.

### Activity 2: Creating Treasure Maps

**Materials:** Construction paper, crayons/markers/colored pencils

**Description:** Children will be asked to design an imaginary treasure map on an island using landforms described in the books (X marks the spot on the land between the *lake*, *ocean*, and *delta*). The teacher might draw out sketches of islands on the construction paper beforehand to save time. Students will share their work at the end and be encouraged to describe their maps using the vocabulary.

# Communication

We provide two types of communication: a classroom posting for students and visitors and a parent letter to be sent home. These are on the next two pages and on the accompanying CD-ROM.

# Landforms Vocabulary Words

boulder

canyon

cliff

delta

desert

gravel

lake

ocean

trench

volcano

Dear Parents:

This week we will be focusing on vocabulary words for Landforms. We will be reading stories and carrying out activities to help your child learn the meanings of these words. By pointing out examples of these words at home and in the community, you can help your child expand his or her vocabulary. This week's words (with simple definitions that children can understand) are as follows:

| | |
|---|---|
| **boulder** | a large, round rock |
| **canyon** | the part of the river with high sides reaching to the sky |
| **cliff** | the edge of a high mountain |
| **delta** | where a river connects to the sea |
| **desert** | a dry place where it doesn't rain a lot |
| **gravel** | small, loose stones or rocks used for paths and roads |
| **lake** | water surrounded by land |
| **ocean** | salty water that covers most of the earth |
| **trench** | a long, skinny hole in the ground |
| **volcano** | a mountain that spits out very hot liquid |

Please post this where you and your child can see it. Thanks!

Sincerely,

Your child's teacher

# 18 Maps and Globes

## Vocabulary

| | |
|---|---|
| atlas | legend |
| compass | map |
| equator | planet |
| globe | pole |
| highway | route |

## New VEhicles—
## N3C Vocabulary Introduction

### Initial Presentation

Find pictures for all vocabulary words listed below as well as the two known words paired with each vocabulary word. The known words should be in children's vocabularies. If not, substitute another from the set of pictures that your students are likely to know. In the large-group setting, show all three pictures (the vocabulary word and the two known words) randomly to the children and ask them, "Which one is _____?" (insert vocabulary word). The children should be able to infer that the vocabulary word refers to the unknown picture among the three. If you wish, the quick definitions can be introduced then as well. All pictures are included in the accompanying CD-ROM.

| Vocabulary words | Known words |
|---|---|
| atlas | bed, bus |
| compass | ball, book |
| equator | coat, dress |
| globe | circle, TV |
| highway | truck, traffic light |
| legend | hotdog, toothbrush |
| map | road, key |
| planet | balloon, king |
| pole | pencil, hammer |
| route | couch, lamp |

### Subsequent Presentation

After the initial presentation the pictures of the known words can be put away. The rest of the week, display only the pictures of the vocabulary words and say to children, "Show me _____" (insert vocabulary word) or "What's the word for this?" (point at picture).

# Quick Definitions

**atlas**  a book of maps

**compass**  something you use to find direction with a needle that always points north

**equator**  an imaginary line that mapmakers draw around the middle of the Earth, halfway between the North and South Poles

**globe**  it looks like our Earth

**highway**  a big wide road where lots of cars drive

**legend**  the part of the map that explains how to use it

**map**  a flat picture of a place that shows things like towns, roads, rivers, and mountains

**planet**  the world we live on

**pole**  the top and bottom of the Earth

**route**  the road or course that you follow to get from one place to another

# CAR Quest

The following are questions that you can ask students about the story you are reading. We suggest reviewing the text beforehand and using sticky notes to mark appropriate places to pause for discussion. The questions are labeled according to the types described in Chapter 3.

## Books

Rabe, T. (2002). *There's a map on my lap: All about maps.* New York: Random House.

Walters, V. (1999). *Are we there yet, Daddy?* New York: Puffin Books.

Page location describes the picture (illustration or photo) that relates to the individual CAR Quest question. Unknown vocabulary words are *italicized*.

### There's a Map on My Lap

**Page location:** First picture, the Cat in the Hat and Thing One and Thing Two arrive.

> **Relate:** Where have you ever used a *map*? What do you use *maps* for?

> **Relate:** If you had a *map* that could take you anywhere in the world, where would you go?

**Page location:** The Cat in the Hat shows one of the children a *globe*.

> **Abstract:** What sorts of thing would you find on a *globe*?

> **Abstract:** Where is the *equator* on the *globe*? If you were to go up into space, could you see the *equator*? Why not?

**Page location:** The Cat in the Hat shows two children a *compass* rose.

> **Competence:** What is the cat pointing to on the *map*?

**Page location:** Thing One and Thing Two hold a *map legend*.

> **Competence:** Show me the *legend* on this *map*?

### Are We There Yet, Daddy?

**Page location:** It is 90 miles to Grandma's house.

> **Competence:** What sorts of things do you see when you travel on a *highway*?

> **Relate:** Have you ever taken a trip on a *highway*? Where did you go?

> **Abstract:** How is a *highway* different than a road?

**Page location:** Driving through a neighborhood, the dad and son are almost there.

    **Competence:** Look at the map here and you can see the *route* that Dad and his son took. Where are some of the things that they will see on their *route* home again?

    **Relate:** Have you ever used a *route* to go somewhere?

    **Abstract:** If you were going to draw a *route* to a place, where would you go?

## Building Bridges— Start 'em Up! Topic

What kinds of landforms are there around where you live?

## New VEhicles— Extension Activities

### Activity 1: Bring in Maps

**Materials:** *Maps* brought in by the children

**Description:** Have the children bring in a *map* of their choosing. It can be from a museum, a zoo, their car, and so forth. Have them describe to other children what is on their *map*.

### Activity 2: All Sorts of Maps and Globes

**Materials:** A *globe*; a variety of *maps* such as world, state, city, topographical, political, museum, amusement park, zoo, subway, bus, road, and treasure maps; Internet *maps*

**Description:** Share the various *maps* and *globes* with the children, talking about what they notice on the *map*, what they think is missing, and how such a *map* might be useful. Place the *maps* in a center, giving children time to explore them. Finally, select two points on the *map* and ask children to come up with a *route* for getting from one place to the other. Vocabulary should be integrated.

# Communication

We provide two types of communication: a classroom posting for students and visitors and a parent letter to be sent home. These are found on the next two pages and on the accompanying CD-ROM.

# Maps and Globes
# Vocabulary Words

atlas

compass

equator

globe

highway

legend

map

planet

pole

route

Dear Parents,

This week we will be focusing on vocabulary words for Maps and Globes. We will be reading stories and carrying out activities to help your child learn the meanings of these words. By pointing out examples of these words at home and in the community, you can help your child expand his or her vocabulary. This week's words (with simple definitions that children can understand) are as follows:

| | |
|---|---|
| atlas | a book of maps |
| compass | something you use to find direction with a needle that always points north |
| equator | an imaginary line that mapmakers draw around the middle of the Earth, halfway between the North and South Poles |
| globe | it looks like our Earth |
| highway | a big wide road where lots of cars drive |
| legend | the part of the map that explains how to use it |
| map | a flat picture of a place that shows things like towns, roads, rivers, and mountains |
| planet | the world we live on |
| pole | the top and bottom of the Earth |
| route | the road or course that you follow to get from one place to another |

Please post this where you and your child can see it. Thanks!

Sincerely,

Your child's teacher

UNIT

**19** **Medieval Times**

## Vocabulary

| | |
|---|---|
| armor | letter |
| castle | library |
| cave | slingshot |
| dragon | sword |
| knight | tunic |

## New VEhicles—
## N3C Vocabulary Introduction

### Initial Presentation

Find pictures for all vocabulary words listed below as well as the two known words paired with each vocabulary word. The known words should be in children's vocabularies. If not, substitute another from the set of pictures that your students are likely to know. In the large-group setting, show all three pictures (the vocabulary word and the two known words) randomly to the children and ask them, "Which one is _____?" (insert vocabulary word). The children should be able to infer that the vocabulary word refers to the unknown picture among the three. If you wish, the quick definitions can be introduced then as well. All pictures are included in the accompanying CD-ROM.

| Vocabulary words | Known words |
|---|---|
| armor | arm, eye |
| castle | bed, bridge |
| cave | circle, clock |
| dragon | butterfly, dinosaur |
| knight | clown, policeman |
| letter | hotdog, toothbrush |
| library | stairs, piano |
| slingshot | slide, scissors |
| sword | spoon, pencil |
| tunic | bed, pants |

### Subsequent Presentation

After the initial presentation the pictures of the known words can be put away. The rest of the week, display only the pictures of the vocabulary words and say to children, "Show me _____" (insert vocabulary word) or "What's the word for this?" (point at picture).

# Quick Definitions

**armor**    something you wear that protects you

**castle**    where a king and queen live

**cave**    a hole in the side of a hill

**dragon**    a pretend monster that blows fire

**knight**    a soldier from long ago that rode on horses and served a king

**letter**    a message written on a piece of paper

**library**    a place where books are kept

**slingshot**    something that shoots small rocks

**sword**    it has a long blade

**tunic**    a long shirt that comes almost to your knees

# CAR Quest

The following are questions that you can ask students about the story you are reading. We suggest reviewing the text beforehand and using sticky notes to mark appropriate places to pause for discussion. The questions are labeled according to the types described in Chapter 3.

## Books

dePaola, T. (1980). *The knight and the dragon.* New York: Paperback Star.

Mayer, M. (1968). *The bravest knight.* New York: Penguin Group.

Page location describes the picture (illustration or photo) that relates to the individual CAR Quest question. Unknown vocabulary words are *italicized*.

### *The Knight and the Dragon*

**Page location:** First illustration, *knight* in the *castle* and *dragon* in his *cave*

   **Abstract:** Why do you think the *knight* would want to fight a *dragon*?

   **Competence:** What is the *knight* wearing?

   **Competence:** Who is bigger, the *knight* or a *dragon*?

**Page location:** The *knight* finds books in the *library*.

   **Relate:** Have you ever taken a visit to a *library*?

**Page location:** The *dragon* reads a book on fighting *knights*.

   **Abstract:** Why does the *dragon* live in a *cave*?

   **Relate:** Have you ever been inside a *cave*?

### *The Bravest Knight*

**Page location:** The boy sharpens a *sword*.

   **Competence:** Where in the picture is the *sword*?

   **Abstract:** Why do you think a *sword* needs to be sharpened?

**Page location:** The boy is dressing up and holding a *slingshot*.

   **Relate:** Where have you seen someone use a *slingshot*?

   **Competence:** What is the *slingshot* made of?

Page location: The brave *knight* pokes the *dragon* with his *sword*.

Relate: Would you want to wear a *tunic* to school?

Abstract: Why would someone want to be a squire for the bravest *knight* and not some other *knight*?

# Building Bridges—
# Start 'em Up! Topic

I wonder what it would be like to be a kid living in medieval times. What do you think? Do you think you would be excited to be living then?

# New VEhicles—
# Extension Activities

## Activity 1: Art Activity—Knight Adventure!

Materials: Picture of a *knight* (provided) for each child, construction paper, scissors, markers/crayons/colored pencils, glue

Description: After giving out the *knight* pictures, the teacher will explain that the children are to imagine an adventure that their *knight* is going on. Where will the *knight* go? What will he or she encounter on the journey? Is the *knight* going to save a prince or princess, or will the children create a companion to come along for the fun? Is the *knight* wearing a *tunic* or *armor*? Will he or she fight a *dragon* and carry a *slingshot* or *sword*? Children should write down their ideas (or draw them) and share their small projects at the end of the activity.

## Activity 2: Skit Activity—Medieval Performance

Materials: Crayons or colored pencils, aluminum foil (for making *armor* and crowns), tape, construction paper, stapler, string, tissue paper (for veils and dresses)

Description: Under the supervision of a teacher, have children begin to formulate an original short story (5 minutes or so) that features medieval characters (e.g., *knights, dragons,* princesses). Select different children to play the parts, and create simple costumes and props (crowns from construction paper, *tunics* from large pieces of white paper tied together with string) using the materials. Have children perform the skit after sufficient time for practice. A good idea might be to split the class into two parts and have the groups perform for each other.

# Communication

We provide two types of communication: a classroom posting for students and visitors and a parent letter to be sent home. These are on the next two pages and on the accompanying CD-ROM.

# Medieval Times
# Vocabulary Words

armor

castle

cave

dragon

knight

letter

library

slingshot

sword

tunic

Dear Parents,

This week we will be focusing on vocabulary words for Medieval Times. We will be reading stories and carrying out activities to help your child learn the meanings of these words. By pointing out examples of these words at home and in the community, you can help your child expand his or her vocabulary. This week's words (with simple definitions that children can understand) are as follows:

| | |
|---|---|
| **armor** | something you wear that protects you |
| **castle** | where a king and queen live |
| **cave** | a hole in the side of a hill |
| **dragon** | a pretend monster that blows fire |
| **knight** | a soldier from long ago that rode on horses and served a king |
| **letter** | a message written on a piece of paper |
| **library** | a place where books are kept |
| **slingshot** | something that shoots small rocks |
| **sword** | it has a long blade |
| **tunic** | a long shirt that comes almost to your knees |

Please post this where you and your child can see it. Thanks!

Sincerely,

Your child's teacher

# Music

## Vocabulary

| | |
|---|---|
| cello | harp |
| clarinet | orchestra |
| conductor | tambourine |
| flute | trombone |
| French horn | trumpet |

## New VEhicles—
## N3C Vocabulary Introduction

### Initial Presentation

Find pictures for all vocabulary words listed below as well as the two known words paired with each vocabulary word. The known words should be in children's vocabularies. If not, substitute another from the set of pictures that your students are likely to know. In the large-group setting, show all three pictures (the vocabulary word and the two known words) randomly to the children and ask them, "Which one is _____?" (insert vocabulary word). The children should be able to infer that the vocabulary word refers to the unknown picture among the three. If you wish, the quick definitions can be introduced then as well. All pictures are included in the accompanying CD-ROM.

| Vocabulary words | Known words |
|---|---|
| cello | banana, carrot |
| clarinet | box, brush |
| conductor | clown, king |
| flute | arm, book |
| French horn | ball, phone |
| harp | chair, toilet |
| orchestra | dress, drum |
| tambourine | square, ear |
| trombone | spoon, piano |
| trumpet | teeth, phone |

### Subsequent Presentation

After the initial presentation the pictures of the known words can be put away. The rest of the week, display only the pictures of the vocabulary words and say to children, "Show me _____" (insert vocabulary word) or "What's the word for this?" (point at picture).

## Quick Definitions

**cello**   a string instrument that sits on the floor

**clarinet**   a long black instrument you blow that has silver keys

**conductor**   the person who leads the orchestra

**flute**   a small silver thing you blow that makes a high sound

**French horn**   a horn that is all tangled up

**harp**   an instrument with lots of strings that you pluck

**orchestra**   people making music together

**tambourine**   a small round instrument you shake and slap to make noise

**trombone**   a brass horn that uses a slide

**trumpet**   a brass horn with three keys

## CAR Quest

The following are questions that you can ask students about the story you are reading. We suggest reviewing the text beforehand and using sticky notes to mark appropriate places to pause for discussion. The questions are labeled according to the types described in Chapter 3.

### Books

Moss, L. (2005). *Zin! Zin! Zin! A violin*. New York: Simon & Schuster Books for Young Readers.

Isadora, R. (1979). *Ben's trumpet*. New York: Scholastic.

Page location describes the picture (illustration or photo) that relates to the individual CAR Quest question. Unknown vocabulary words are *italicized*.

### *Zin! Zin! Zin! A Violin*

**Page location:** Three musicians, one playing a *trombone*, one playing *trumpet*, and one playing a *French horn*

    **Abstract:** Why do you think the *French horn* is curled in a circle?

**Page location:** A Chinese woman plays the *flute*.

    **Relate:** Would you like to play a *flute* someday?

    **Competence:** Could you find the man playing the *French horn*?

**Page location:** A woman playing a *harp* floats in the air.

    **Competence:** Can someone count how many strings are on the *cello*?

    **Abstract:** Why do you think the *harp* has so many strings?

    **Relate:** Have you ever seen a *harp* before in real life?

### *Ben's Trumpet*

**Page location:** Ben listens to the musicians practice at the Zig Zag Jazz Club.

    **Competence:** Can you find the *trumpet* in the picture?

    **Competence:** Can you tell who is playing the *trombone*?

    **Relate:** Would you like to learn to play a *trombone* or a *trumpet*? Why?

**Page location:** The musician turns and twists as he plays the *trumpet*.

    **Abstract:** Why do you think the man playing the *trumpet* moves like this?

    **Relate:** How would you move if you were playing a *trumpet*? What about a *trombone*?

**Page location:** The musician shows Ben how to play the *trumpet*.

    **Abstract:** Why are Ben's cheeks puffed when he plays the *trumpet*?

# Building Bridges—
# Start 'em Up! Topic

I love music. What kind of music do you like to listen to? What instruments do you hear with that?

# New VEhicles—
# Extension Activities

## Activity 1: Instrument Families

**Materials:** Pictures of instruments (provided)

**Description:** Students will be presented with pictures of each instrument (all nine laid out on the table) and asked to place them into families. Encourage the children to talk about why they put the different instruments together. Afterward, arrange the instruments into wind, brass, or string families and provide an additional point of view if this has not already been mentioned. Focus on how the sum total of all of the instruments forms an *orchestra*.

## Activity 2: Sound Guessing

**Materials:** Computer with speakers or CD/audio player/stereo, instrument sound recordings (obtained from http://www.dsokids.com/2001/instrumentchart.htm), paper, pencils/crayons

**Description:** Students will listen to different sounds and try to identify which instrument makes that sound. Students will draw what they believe to be the correct instrument while the music is playing and share when they have completed their work.

# Communication

We provide two types of communication: a classroom posting for students and visitors and a parent letter to be sent home. These are on the next two pages and on the accompanying CD-ROM.

# Music Vocabulary Words

cello

clarinet

conductor

flute

French horn

harp

orchestra

tambourine

trombone

trumpet

Dear Parents:

This week we will be focusing on vocabulary words for Music. We will be reading stories and carrying out activities to help your child learn the meanings of these words. By pointing out examples of these words at home and in the community, you can help your child expand his or her vocabulary. This week's words (with simple definitions that children can understand) are as follows:

| | |
|---|---|
| cello | a string instrument that sits on the floor |
| clarinet | a long black instrument you blow that has silver keys |
| conductor | the person who leads the orchestra |
| flute | a small silver thing you blow that makes a high sound |
| French horn | a horn that is all tangled up |
| harp | an instrument with lots of strings that you pluck |
| orchestra | people making music together |
| tambourine | a small round instrument you shake and slap to make noise |
| trombone | a brass horn that uses a slide |
| trumpet | a brass horn with three keys |

Please post this where you and your child can see it. Thanks!

Sincerely,

Your child's teacher

UNIT
**21**

# Primary Land Uses
## Farming and Fishing

## New VEhicles—
## N3C Vocabulary Introduction

### Initial Presentation

Find pictures for all vocabulary words listed below as well as the two known words paired with each vocabulary word. The known words should be in children's vocabularies. If not, substitute another from the set of pictures that your students are likely to know. In the large-group setting, show all three pictures (the vocabulary word and the two known words) randomly to the children and ask them, "Which one is _____?" (insert vocabulary word). The children should be able to infer that the vocabulary word refers to the unknown picture among the three. If you wish, the quick definitions can be introduced then as well. All pictures are included in the accompanying CD-ROM.

| Vocabulary words | Known words |
|---|---|
| bait | bird, hotdog |
| barn | box, chicken |
| canoe | bus, truck |
| fishing pole | bread, carrot |
| hay | sandwich, horse |
| hook | banana, teeth |
| lure | cake, fish |
| mower | TV, toilet |
| plow | boot, saw |
| thermos | apple, cheese |

### Subsequent Presentation

After the initial presentation the pictures of the known words can be put away. The rest of the week, display only the pictures of the vocabulary words and say to children, "Show me _____" (insert vocabulary word) or "What's the word for this?" (point at picture).

# Quick Definitions

**bait**    a worm used to catch fish

**barn**    a type of house that farm animals live in

**canoe**    a long, thin, open boat

**fishing pole**    a long stick that you use to catch fish

**hay**    dried grass used for feeding farm animals

**hook**    something you use to catch fish that the fish bites down on

**lure**    something you use to catch fish

**mower**    you use it to cut grass

**plow**    a tool for breaking up the dirt

**thermos**    something that you can hold soup or coffee in to keep it hot

 # CAR Quest

The following are questions that you can ask students about the story you are reading. We suggest reviewing the text beforehand and using sticky notes to mark appropriate places to pause for discussion. The questions are labeled according to the types described in Chapter 3.

## Books

Gibbons, G. (1988). *Farming*. New York: Holiday House.

Creech, S. (2000). *Fishing in the air*. New York: Joanna Cotler.

Page location describes the picture (illustration or photo) that relates to the individual CAR Quest question. Unknown vocabulary words are *italicized*.

### Farming

**Page location:** As spring arrives two farmers walk to the *barn*.

  **Competence:** What's in the *barn*?

  **Relate:** Have you ever been to a *barn*?

**Page location:** The farmer uses a tractor to *plow* the field.

  **Relate:** Has anyone ever seen a *plow*?

  **Abstract:** How does the *plow* turn over the soil?

**Page location:** The farmer harvests the *hay*.

  **Competence:** What is the *mower* cutting?

  **Abstract:** Why do you think they want to cut the *hay*?

### Fishing in the Air

**Page location:** First picture, the boy and his father dig up some worms to use as *bait*.

  **Competence:** What color is the worm the father uses for *bait*?

  **Abstract:** Why would a fisherman use a worm as *bait*?

**Page location:** The boy and his father pack for their fishing trip.

  **Relate:** What would you put in a *thermos*?

**Page location:** The boy and his father arrive at the fishing spot and get their *fishing poles* ready.

**Competence:** The boy's feather is a *lure*. What color is his *lure*?

**Abstract:** Why do you think the boy had no *hook* on his line?

**Relate:** Has anyone ever used a *fishing pole*?

# Building Bridges—
# Start 'em Up! Topic

Have you ever been fishing? What did you bring with you?

# New VEhicles—
# Extension Activities

## Activity 1: Farm Art

**Materials:** Paper, pencils/markers/crayons

**Description:** Students will be asked to create their own farms using the vocabulary for farming (Where is the *barn*? Does your farm have a *plow*? Will the animals have *hay* to eat?). Sharing time should be allotted.

## Activity 2: Let's Go Fishing

**Materials:** Stick (for *fishing pole*); yarn or string (for fishing line); one magnet; eight paperclips; six fish cut out of construction paper; pictures of *fishing pole, hook, canoe, lure, bait, thermos* (supplied)

**Description:** Create a *fishing pole* by attaching a magnet to the end of a string. Attach the string to the end of the stick that will serve as the pole. Write a vocabulary word from the fishing unit (*fishing pole, hook, canoe, lure, bait, thermos*) on each fish. Attach a paperclip to each fish. Have students try to catch the fish by pulling them up using the *fishing pole*. Have students match the word to the picture from the unit supplied.

# Communication

We provide two types of communication: a classroom posting for students and visitors and a parent letter to be sent home. These are on the next two pages and on the accompanying CD-ROM.

# Primary Land Uses: Farming and Fishing Vocabulary Words

bait

barn

canoe

fishing pole

hay

hook

lure

mower

plow

thermos

Dear Parents,

This week we will be focusing on vocabulary words for Primary Land Uses: Farming and Fishing. We will be reading stories and carrying out activities to help your child learn the meanings of these words. By pointing out examples of these words at home and in the community, you can help your child expand his or her vocabulary. This week's words (with simple definitions that children can understand) are as follows:

| | |
|---|---|
| **bait** | a worm used to catch fish |
| **barn** | a type of house that farm animals live in |
| **canoe** | a long, thin, open boat |
| **fishing pole** | a long stick that you use to catch fish |
| **hay** | dried grass used for feeding farm animals |
| **hook** | something you use to catch fish that the fish bites down on |
| **lure** | something you use to catch fish |
| **mower** | you use it to cut grass |
| **plow** | a tool for breaking up the dirt |
| **thermos** | something that you can hold soup or coffee in to keep it hot |

Please post this where you and your child can see it. Thanks!

Sincerely,

Your child's teacher

## Vocabulary

| | |
|---|---|
| branch | shade |
| bud | shed |
| gold | stall |
| horseshoe | stem |
| nest | wreath |

## New VEhicles— N3C Vocabulary Introduction

### Initial Presentation

Find pictures for all vocabulary words listed below as well as the two known words paired with each vocabulary word. The known words should be in children's vocabularies. If not, substitute another from the set of pictures that your students are likely to know. In the large-group setting, show all three pictures (the vocabulary word and the two known words) randomly to the children and ask them, "Which one is _____?" (insert vocabulary word). The children should be able to infer that the vocabulary word refers to the unknown picture among the three. If you wish, the quick definitions can be introduced then as well. All pictures are included in the accompanying CD-ROM.

| Vocabulary words | Known words |
|---|---|
| branch | butterfly, dinosaur |
| bud | balloon, bottle |
| gold | corn, pants |
| horseshoe | boot, glasses |
| nest | chair, tree |
| shade | orange, lamp |
| shed | window, table |
| stall | square, horse |
| stem | scissors, lamp |
| wreath | triangle, door |

### Subsequent Presentation

After the initial presentation the pictures of the known words can be put away. The rest of the week, display only the pictures of the vocabulary words and say to children, "Show me _____" (insert vocabulary word) or "What's the word for this?" (point at picture).

# Quick Definitions

**branch**  the arms of the tree that reach to the sky

**bud**  a baby flower

**gold**  a dark yellow color

**horseshoe**  metal shoe that horses wear

**nest**  a home for baby birds

**shade**  place under a tree or next to the house where the sun isn't shining; usually feels a little cooler

**shed**  a small building often used to store things

**stall**  a little room for horses or cows in a barn

**stem**  the part of the plant that holds the flower up

**wreath**  a circle of flowers that hangs on the door

# CAR Quest

The following are questions that you can ask students about the story you are reading. We suggest reviewing the text beforehand and using sticky notes to mark appropriate places to pause for discussion. The questions are labeled according to the types described in Chapter 3.

## Books

Provensen, A., & Provensen, M. (2001). *The year at Maple Hill Farm*. New York: Aladdin.

Gibbons, G. (1984). *The seasons of Arnold's apple tree*. New York: Harcourt Brace Jovanovich.

Page location describes the picture (illustration or photo) that relates to the individual CAR Quest question. Unknown vocabulary words are *italicized*.

### *The Year at Maple Hill Farm*

**Page location:** Various birds are sitting in their *nests*.

> **Competence:** How many baby chicks have hatched in the *nest*?

> **Abstract:** Why is the big bird laying an egg in the little *nest*?

**Page location:** On a hot summer's night, the men load bales of hay into the barn.

> **Competence:** Can you point out the goose that found shelter in the *shed*?

**Page location:** The cows lie under a *shady* tree.

> **Relate:** When it is hot on the playground, where do we find *shade*?

**Page location:** The blacksmith tends to the horse.

> **Abstract:** The blacksmith is putting on *horseshoes*. Why do the horses wear shoes?

**Page location:** Two people get ready to ride their horses in the rain.

> **Relate:** Would you want to live in a horse *stall*?

### *The Seasons of Arnold's Apple Tree*

**Page location:** First picture, Arnold is perched on the top of the apple tree.

> **Competence:** How many *branches* does the tree have?

> **Relate:** Have you ever climbed a tree's *branches*?

**Page location:** Arnold inspects the new leaves and *buds*.

> **Abstract:** What do you think the *buds* will grow into?

**Page location:** Arnold makes a *wreath* to decorate the tree.

    **Abstract:** If you were going to make a *wreath*, what would you make it out of?

    **Relate:** Do you think the *wreath* is pretty hanging from the tree?

**Page location:** Arnold rakes the leaves under the apple tree.

    **Competence:** How many piles of *gold* leaves has Arnold made?

# Building Bridges— Start 'em Up! Topic

What is your favorite season? Why?

# New VEhicles— Extension Activities

### Activity 1: Create a Seasons Book

**Materials:** Two sheets of paper for each student, markers and crayons

**Description:** Have the children divide each paper in half with a line. On one side write fall and on the other side write winter. On the other page, write spring on one side and summer on the other. Have each child draw different events that take place during different times of the year (e.g., *buds* bloom and chicks hatch in *nests* in the spring, leaves turn the color *gold* in the fall, animals stay in a *shed* or *stall* during the winter when it is cold). The children can work in small groups to decide what they would like to draw. Staple the pages together at the end to form a four-page book.

### Activity 2: Leaves on the Tree

**Materials:** Paper of different colors found in nature at various times of year (e.g., green, yellow, gold, brown), glue stick, pencil

**Description:** Have children draw four different stick trees like this:

Cut the construction paper to make leaves for the trees. Have the children write spring, summer, fall, and winter at the top of the quadrants of the paper. Have them glue the appropriate leaves that go along with the season on their trees (e.g., *gold* for fall, white snow for winter). Extra leaves can be used for making construction paper *wreaths*. Emphasis should be placed on using the vocabulary words *branch, bud, wreath, gold, shade,* and *nest.*

# Communication

We provide two types of communication: a classroom posting for students and visitors and a parent letter to be sent home. These are on the next two pages and on the accompanying CD-ROM.

# Seasons Vocabulary Words

branch

bud

gold

horseshoe

nest

shade

shed

stall

stem

wreath

Dear Parents:

This week we will be focusing on vocabulary words for Seasons. We will be reading stories and carrying out activities to help your child learn the meanings of these words. By pointing out examples of these words at home and in the community, you can help your child expand his or her vocabulary. This week's words (with simple definitions that children can understand) are as follows:

| | |
|---|---|
| branch | the arm of the tree that reaches to the sky |
| bud | a baby flower |
| gold | a dark yellow color |
| horseshoe | metal shoe that horses wear |
| nest | a home for baby birds |
| shade | place under a tree or next to the house where the sun isn't shining; usually feels a little cooler |
| shed | a small building often used to store things |
| stall | a little room for horses or cows in a barn |
| stem | the part of the plant that holds the flower up |
| wreath | a circle of flowers that hangs on the door |

Please post this where you and your child can see it. Thanks!

Sincerely,

Your child's teacher

UNIT

# **23** Weather

## Vocabulary

| | |
|---|---|
| cloud | monsoon |
| flood | puddle |
| forecast | seashore |
| lighthouse | thermometer |
| lightning | waves |

## New VEhicles—
## N3C Vocabulary Introduction

### Initial Presentation

Find pictures for all vocabulary words listed below as well as the two known words paired with each vocabulary word. The known words should be in children's vocabularies. If not, substitute another from the set of pictures that your students are likely to know. In the large-group setting, show all three pictures (the vocabulary word and the two known words) randomly to the children and ask them, "Which one is _____?" (insert vocabulary word). The children should be able to infer that the vocabulary word refers to the unknown picture among the three. If you wish, the quick definitions can be introduced then as well. All pictures are included in the accompanying CD-ROM.

| Vocabulary word | Known words |
|---|---|
| cloud | bread, clock |
| flood | bib, rain |
| forecast | plane, paper |
| lighthouse | window, glasses |
| lightning | plane, ear |
| monsoon | elephant, house |
| puddle | ring, hamburger |
| seashore | nose, guitar |
| thermometer | bottle, orange |
| waves | slide, run |

### Subsequent Presentation

After the initial presentation the pictures of the known words can be put away. The rest of the week, display only the pictures of the vocabulary words and say to children, "Show me _____" (insert vocabulary word) or "What's the word for this?" (point at picture).

# Quick Definitions

**cloud**  a white thing in the sky that can look like fluffy cotton balls

**flood**  when there is so much water that the lakes and rivers cannot hold it anymore

**forecast**  something that tells you what the weather is going to be like

**lighthouse**  a tall skinny building with a flashing light at the top

**lightning**  a flash of light in the sky when it is raining out

**monsoon**  a very strong wind that blows across the ocean bringing very heavy rains

**puddle**  a small pool of water

**seashore**  the sandy land next to the sea

**thermometer**  it tells you how hot or cold something is

**waves**  big moving splashes of water you see in the ocean

# CAR Quest

The following are questions that you can ask students about the story you are reading. We suggest reviewing the text beforehand and using sticky notes to mark appropriate places to pause for discussion. The questions are labeled according to the types described in Chapter 3.

## Books

Bridwell, N. (1995). *Clifford and the big storm.* New York: Scholastic.

Krishnaswami, U. (2003). *Monsoon.* New York: Farrar, Straus and Giroux.

Page location describes the picture (illustration or photo) that relates to the individual CAR Quest question. Unknown vocabulary words are *italicized*.

### *Clifford and the Big Storm*

**Page location:** First picture, Emily Elizabeth and Clifford visit grandma.

  **Competence:** What kinds of things are at the *seashore*?

**Page location:** As Clifford is making a pile of sand, *lightning* strikes the *lighthouse*.

  **Relate:** Is anyone here scared of *lightning*?

  **Abstract:** Why might *waves* be dangerous during a storm?

**Page location:** The *lighthouse* is burning.

  **Competence:** Where is the *lighthouse*?

  **Abstract:** Why did *lightning* make the *lighthouse* catch fire?

  **Relate:** Has anyone ever been to a *lighthouse* before?

### *Monsoon*

**Page location:** First picture, the family eats breakfast at the table.

  **Abstract:** During a *monsoon* do you think there is a little or a lot of rain?

**Page location:** Mommy and the children look in the sky.

  **Relate:** Has anyone ever been in a *flood* or seen one on TV? Tell us about it.

**Page location:** Nani reads the boy a book and the girl makes paper boats.

> **Relate:** Have any of you played in a *puddle* recently?

> **Competence:** What is the little girl making to float on the *puddles*?

**Page location:** Mommy and the children walk under a tree on a city street.

> **Competence:** What colors are the *clouds* in the sky?

# Building Bridges— Start 'em Up! Topic

What's the weather like today? Do you like this kind of weather? Why?

# New VEhicles— Extension Activities

### Activity 1: Preparing for the Weather

**Materials:** Pictures of weather words (*waves, lightning, monsoon, flood, puddle, cloud, thermometer, forecast*)

**Description:** Divide students into pairs. Give each pair a weather word picture. Have them talk about what they should do to get ready for that weather (e.g., what they should wear, what they should avoid).

### Activity 2: Read the Weekly Forecast

**Materials:** Some newspaper weather sections. Try to collect a variety of weather conditions (e.g., thunderstorms, *cloudy*, sunny, tornado) like the pictorial ones found in USA Today or printed online weather forecasts from weather.com

**Description:** Draw or show general weather condition pictures on the board (e.g., a *cloud* with *lightning*, a rain *cloud*, wind). Explain what each symbol means. Divide students into small groups and give each group a newspaper weather section. Ask the students to identify the weather forecast and then present the week's weather conditions based on their particular newspaper.

# Communication

We provide two types of communication: a classroom posting for students and visitors and a parent letter to be sent home. These are on the next two pages and on the accompanying CD-ROM.

# Weather Vocabulary Words

cloud

flood

forecast

lighthouse

lightning

monsoon

puddle

seashore

thermometer

waves

*PAVEd for Success: Building Vocabulary and Language Development in Young Learners,* by Claire E. Hamilton & Paula J. Schwanenflugel.
Copyright © 2011 by Paul H. Brookes Publishing Co., Inc. All rights reserved.

Dear Parents:

This week we will be focusing on vocabulary words for Weather. We will be reading stories and carrying out activities to help your child learn the meanings of these words. By pointing out examples of these words at home and in the community, you can help your child expand his or her vocabulary. This week's words (with simple definitions that children can understand) are as follows:

| | |
|---|---|
| cloud | a white thing in the sky that can look like fluffy cotton balls |
| flood | when there is so much water that the lakes and rivers cannot hold it anymore |
| forecast | something that tells you what the weather is going to be like |
| lighthouse | a tall skinny building with a flashing light at the top |
| lightning | a flash of light in the sky when it is raining out |
| monsoon | a very strong wind that blows across the ocean bringing very heavy rains |
| puddle | a small pool of water |
| seashore | the sandy land next to the sea |
| thermometer | it tells you how hot or cold something is |
| waves | big moving splashes of water you see in the ocean |

Please post this where you and your child can see it. Thanks!

Sincerely,

Your child's teacher

## Vocabulary

| | |
|---|---|
| burrow | owl |
| fireplace | skates |
| icicle | sled |
| mitten | snowflake |
| mole | wool |

## New VEhicles— N3C Vocabulary Introduction

### Initial Presentation

Find pictures for all vocabulary words listed below as well as the two known words paired with each vocabulary word. The known words should be in children's vocabularies. If not, substitute another from the set of pictures that your students are likely to know. In the large-group setting, show all three pictures (the vocabulary word and the two known words) randomly to the children and ask them, "Which one is _____?" (insert vocabulary word). The children should be able to infer that the vocabulary word refers to the unknown picture among the three. If you wish, the quick definitions can be introduced then as well. All pictures are included in the accompanying CD-ROM.

| Vocabulary words | Known words |
|---|---|
| burrow | box, cup |
| fireplace | stairs, paper |
| icicle | triangle, paper |
| mitten | boot, shirt |
| mole | cat, fish |
| owl | cat, egg |
| skates | bike, swing |
| sled | snowman, slide |
| snowflake | sun, hat |
| wool | sock, frog |

### Subsequent Presentation

After the initial presentation the pictures of the known words can be put away. The rest of the week, display only the pictures of the vocabulary words and say to children, "Show me _____" (insert vocabulary word) or "What's the word for this?" (point at picture).

# Quick Definitions

**burrow**   the place underground where some animals live in the winter

**fireplace**   where our parents can make a fire in the house to keep us warm

**icicle**   ice hanging from trees or houses

**mitten**   warm gloves for your hands

**mole**   a tiny little mousy animal that lives in the ground

**owl**   a bird that wakes up at night and says, "Hoot, hoot!"

**skates**   shoes used on ice

**sled**   a toy that you use to slide down a snowy hill

**snowflake**   a single piece of snow

**wool**   fabric made from sheep fur

# CAR Quest

The following are questions that you can ask students about the story you are reading. We suggest reviewing the text beforehand and using sticky notes to mark appropriate places to pause for discussion. The questions are labeled according to the types described in Chapter 3.

## Books

Brett, J. (1989). *The mitten.* New York: Scholastic.

Fowler, A. (1991). *How do you know it's winter?* Chicago: Children's Press.

Page location describes the picture (illustration or photo) that relates to the individual CAR Quest question. Unknown vocabulary words are *italicized*.

### The Mitten

**Page location:** First picture, a boy is jumping in the snow.

> **Relate:** Have you ever worn a pair of *mittens* before?

**Page location:** The boy brings *wool* to Baba, his grandmother.

> **Abstract:** Why is Baba, the grandmother, sitting close to the *fireplace*?

> **Competence:** What color is the *wool* the boy, Niki, brings to his grandmother?

**Page location:** Niki, the boy, climbs a tree.

> **Abstract:** Will it be easy to find the white *mitten* in the snow? Why?

**Page location:** In the field a *mole* finds the *mitten*.

> **Competence:** Where are the tracks made by the *mole*?

> **Relate:** The *mole burrows* in the *mitten* to get warm. When it's cold, what do you *burrow* into to get warm?

### How Do You Know It's Winter?

**Page location:** People *skate* on the pond.

> **Competence:** Where are the people *skating*?

> **Relate:** Where could we *skate* around here if it were cold enough?

> **Abstract:** Do you think it is easy or hard to wear *skates* on the ice? Why?

**Page location:** Children *sled* down a hill.

    **Competence:** How many children are riding on the *sled*?

    **Relate:** If it was snowing here, where would you take your *sled*?

**Page location:** A *snowflake*

    **Abstract:** Could we count how many *snowflakes* were used to make the snowman?

## Building Bridges—
## Start 'em Up! Topic

What did you do the last time it snowed?

## New VEhicles—
## Extension Activities

### Activity 1: Burrow into the Mitten

**Materials:** Pictures of *mitten*, rabbit, hedgehog, *mole, owl,* mouse

**Description:** Give each child a *mitten* and have him or her cut it out and staple or tape matching sides together. Talk about how we cover ourselves with sweaters, *mittens*, and coats, but animals grow more fur and eventually *burrow* into a warm place in the ground to hibernate. Have them go around in a circle and take turns describing which animal they are going to put in the *mitten* first, second, and so forth, and why they chose it. Have the children put the animal pictures inside the *mitten* to keep the animals warm.

### Activity 2: Snowy Art

**Materials:** Piece of blue construction paper, piece of white construction paper (whole), white construction paper (torn into lots of different-size pieces), glue, pens

**Description:** Have each child design a snowy scene. They can find three pieces of construction paper for a snowman, a piece for a snowball and *icicles*, and some little pieces for *snowflakes*. If they like they can draw features on the snowman and also add a hedgehog and rabbit. Students could also be shown how to fold the whole white paper many times to make a *snowflake*. The finished product should be a unique *snowflake*, and attention should be focused on how—as with real *snowflakes*—each flake is different from the others.

# Communication

We provide two types of communication: a classroom posting for students and visitors and a parent letter to be sent home. These are on the next two pages and on the accompanying CD-ROM.

# Winter Vocabulary Words

burrow

fireplace

icicle

mitten

mole

owl

skates

sled

snowflake

wool

Dear Parents:

This week we will be focusing on vocabulary words for Winter. We will be reading stories and carrying out activities to help your child learn the meanings of these words. By pointing out examples of these words at home and in the community, you can help your child expand his or her vocabulary. This week's words (with simple definitions that children can understand) are as follows:

| | |
|---|---|
| burrow | the place underground where some animals live in the winter |
| fireplace | where our parents can make a fire in the house to keep us warm |
| icicle | ice hanging from trees or houses |
| mitten | warm glove for your hand |
| mole | a tiny little mousy animal that lives in the ground |
| owl | a bird that wakes up at night and says, "Hoot, hoot!" |
| skates | shoes used on ice |
| sled | a toy that you use to slide down a snowy hill |
| snowflake | a single piece of snow |
| wool | fabric made from sheep fur |

Please post this where you and your child can see it. Thanks!

Sincerely,

Your child's teacher

*PAVEd for Success: Building Vocabulary and Language Development in Young Learners*, by Claire E. Hamilton & Paula J. Schwanenflugel.
Copyright © 2011 by Paul H. Brookes Publishing Co., Inc. All rights reserved.

# Children's Literature Included in the Units
## Spanish titles are noted when available.

Allen, J., & Humphries, T. (2000). *Are you a spider?* London: Kingfisher. Spanish: *Eres una araña?* New York: Houghton Mifflin.

Allen, J., & Humphries, T. (2003). *Are you a ladybug?* London: Kingfisher.

Bang, M. (1999). *When Sophie gets angry—really, really angry….* New York: Blue Sky Press. Spanish: *Cuando Sofia se enoja, se enoja de veras.* New York: Scholastic en Español.

Bauer, M. (2006). *Wonders of America: The Grand Canyon.* New York: Aladdin Paperbacks.

Branley, F. (1996). *What makes a magnet?* New York: HarperCollins.

Brett, J. (1989). *The mitten.* New York: Scholastic.

Bridwell, N. (1995). *Clifford and the big storm.* New York: Scholastic.

Bridwell, N. (2005). *Clifford the firehouse dog.* New York: Scholastic. Spanish: *Clifford, el perro bombero.* St. Louis: Turtleback.

Cain, J. (2000). *The way I feel.* Seattle: Parenting Press. Spanish: *Asi me siento yo.* Seattle: Parenting Press.

Carle, E. (1986). *Papa, please get the moon for me.* New York: Simon & Schuster Books for Young Readers. Spanish: *Papa, por favor, consigueme la luna.* Madrid, Spain: Kokinos.

Christelow, E. (2004). *Five little monkeys bake a birthday cake.* New York: Houghton Mifflin. Spanish: *Cinco monitos hacen un pastel de cumpleaños.* New York: HMH Books.

Creech, S. (2000). *Fishing in the air.* New York: Joanna Cotler.

Demarest, C.L. (2001). *Firefighters A to Z.* New York: Scholastic.

dePaola, T. (1980). *The knight and the dragon.* New York: Paperback Star.

Fowler, A. (1991). *How do you know it's winter?* Chicago: Children's Press. Spanish: *Como sabes que es invierno?* Chicago: Children's Press.

Fowler, A. (1995). *The earth is mostly ocean.* New York: Scholastic.

Garrett, G. (2004). *Solids, liquids, and gases.* Chicago: Children's Press.

Gibbons, G. (1984). *The seasons of Arnold's apple tree.* New York: Harcourt Brace Jovanovich.

Gibbons, G. (1988). *Farming.* New York: Holiday House.

Glaser, L. (1992). *Wonderful worms.* New York: Scholastic.

Green, J. (2002). *Why should I protect nature?* New York: Barron's.

Guarino, D. (1989). *Is your mama a llama?* New York: Scholastic Press. Spanish: *Tu mamá es una llama?* New York: Scholastic en Español.

Hunter, R. (1999). *Cross a bridge.* New York: Scholastic.

Isadora, R. (1979). *Ben's trumpet.* New York: Scholastic.

Katz, B. (1999). *Make way for tooth decay.* New York: Scholastic.

Krishnaswami, U. (2003). *Monsoon.* New York: Farrar, Straus and Giroux.

Louise, T. (2007). *When I grow up.* New York: Abrams Books for Young Readers.

Mayer, M. (1968). *The bravest knight.* New York: Penguin Group.

Mayer, M. (2001). *Just going to the dentist.* New York: Penguin Group.

Morris, A. (1990). *On the go.* New York: Scholastic.

Moss, L. (2005). *Zin! Zin! Zin! A violin.* New York: Simon & Schuster Books for Young Readers.

Neitzel, S. (2000). *I'm taking a trip on my train.* New York: Scholastic.

Potter, B. (2004). *The tale of Peter Rabbit.* New York: Grosset & Dunlap. Spanish: *El cuento de Pedro, el conejo.* Mineola, NY: Dover.

Priceman, M. (1994). *How to make an apple pie and see the world.* New York: Alfred A. Knopf.

Provensen, A., & Provensen, M. (2001). *The year at Maple Hill Farm.* New York: Aladdin.

Rabe, T. (2002). *There's a map on my lap: All about maps.* New York: Random House.

Rockwell, A. (2001). *Career day.* New York: Scholastic.

Rockwell, A. (2001). *Welcome to kindergarten.* New York: Walker & Company.

Rosinsky, N. (2003). *Magnets: Pulling together, pushing apart.* Minneapolis, MN: Picture Window Books. Spanish: *Imanes/Magnets: Atraen y rechazan.* Minneapolis, MN: Picture Window Books.

Sherman, J. (2004). *Sunshine: A book about sunlight.* Minneapolis, MN: Picture Window Books.

Showers, P. (1994). *Where does the garbage go?* New York: Harper Trophy.

Simon, S. (2002). *Baby animals.* San Francisco: Chronicle Books.

Stewart, S. (2000). *The gardener.* New York: Farrar Straus Giroux. Spanish: *Bienvenidos a kindergarten!* Doral, FL: Santillana USA.

Tokuda, Y. (2006). *I'm a pill bug.* San Diego: Kane/Miller.

Walters, V. (1999). *Are we there yet, daddy?* New York: Puffin Books.

Wing, N. (2005). *The night before kindergarten.* New York: Grosset & Dunlap.

Ziefert, H. (2005). *From Kalamazoo to Timbuktu.* Maplewood, NJ: Blue Apple Books.

Zoehfeld, K. (1998). *What is the world made of?* New York: HarperCollins.

# References

Anderson, R.C., & Pearson, P.D. (1984). A schema-theoretic view of basic processes in reading comprehension. In P.D. Pearson (Ed.), *Handbook of reading research* (pp. 255–291). New York: Longman.

Aud, S., Fox, M.A., & Kewal-Ramani, A. (2010). *Status and trends in the education of racial and ethnic groups* (Publication No. 2010015). Washington, DC: National Center for Education Statistics.

Auer, E.T., & Bernstein, L.E. (2008). Estimating when and how words are acquired: A natural experiment on the development of the mental lexicon. *Journal of Speech, Language, and Hearing Research, 51,* 750–758.

Balota, D., Milotti, M., & Cortese, M.J. (2001). Subjective frequency estimates for 2,938 monosyllabic words. *Memory & Cognition, 29,* 639–647.

Beck, I.L., & McKeown, M.G. (2001). Text talk: Capturing the benefits of read-aloud experiences for young children. *The Reading Teacher, 55,* 10–20.

Beck, I.L., McKeown, M.G., & Kucan, L. (2002). *Bringing words to life: Robust vocabulary instruction.* New York: Guilford Press.

Berlin, B. (1992). *Ethnobiological classification: Principles of categorization of plants and animals in traditional societies.* Princeton, NJ: Princeton University Press.

Biemiller, A. (2001). Teaching vocabulary: Early, direct, and sequential. *American Educator, 25*(1), 24–28.

Bracken, S.S. (2005). Oral language and reading: Reply to Bracken. *Developmental Psychology, 41,* 1000–1002.

Bradley, R.H., Corwyn, R.F., McAdoo, H.P., & Coll, C.G. (2001). The home environments of children in the United States: Part I. Variations by age, ethnicity, and poverty status. *Child Development, 72,* 1844–1867.

Brewer, W.F., & Lichtenstein, E.H. (1982). Stories are to entertain: A structural-affect theory of stories. *Journal of Pragmatics, 6,* 473–486.

Browder, D.M., Gibbs, S.L., Ahlgrim-Delzell, L., Courtade, G., Mraz, M., & Flowers, C. (2009). Literacy for students with severe developmental disabilities: What should we teach and what should we hope to achieve? *Remedial and Special Education, 30*(5), 269–282.

Bus, A.G., van IJzendoorn, M.H., & Pellegrini, A.D. (1995). Joint book reading makes for success in learning to read: A meta-analysis on intergenerational transmission of literacy. *Review of Educational Research, 65,* 1–21.

Chamberlain, J., & Leal, D. (1999). Caldecott Medal books and readability levels: Not just "picture" books. *The Reading Teacher, 52,* 898–902.

Clymer, T.L. (1963). The utility of phonic generalizations in the primary grades. *The Reading Teacher, 16,* 252–258.

Copple, C., & Bredekamp, S. (2009). *Developmentally appropriate practice in early childhood programs.* Washington, DC: National Association for the Education of Young Children.

Crowe, L.K., Norris, J.A., & Hoffman, P.R. (2004). Training caregivers to facilitate communicative participation of preschool children with language impairments during storybook reading. *Journal of Communication Disorders, 37,* 177–196.

Curenton, S.M., & Justice, L.M. (2004). African American and Caucasian preschoolers' use of decontextualized language: Literate language features in oral narratives. *Language, Speech, and Hearing Services in Schools, 35,* 240–253.

DeMarie, D., Aloise-Young, P., Prideaux, C. Muransky-Doran, & Gerda, J. (2004). College students' memory for vocabulary in their majors: evidence for a nonlinear relation between knowledge and memory. *Canadian Journal of Experimental Psychology, 58*(3), 181–195.

DeThorne, L.S., Petrill, S.A., Schatschneider, C., & Cutting, L. (2010). Conversational language use as a predictor of early reading development: Language history as a moderating variable. *Journal of Speech, Language, and Hearing Research, 53,* 209–223.

Dickinson, D.K. (2001). Book reading in preschool classrooms: Is recommended practice common? In D.K. Dickinson & P.O. Tabors (Eds.), *Beginning literacy with language: Young children learning at home and school* (pp. 175–204). Baltimore: Paul H. Brookes Publishing Co.

Dickinson, D.K., Cote, L.R., & Smith, M.W. (1993). Learning vocabulary in preschool: Social and discourse contexts affecting vocabulary growth. In C. Daiute (Ed.), *New directions for child development series: Vol. 61. The development of literacy through social interaction* (pp. 67–78). San Francisco: Jossey-Bass.

Dickinson, D.K., McCabe, A., Anastasopoulos, L., Peisner-Feinberg, E.S., & Poe, M.D. (2003). The comprehensive language approach to early literacy: The interrelationships among vocabulary, phonological sensitivity, and print knowledge among preschool-aged children. *Journal of Educational Psychology, 95*, 465–481.

Dickinson, D. K., McCabe, A., & Sprague, K. (2001). The teacher rating of oral language and literacy (TROLL): A research-based tool, CIERA Report #3-016. Ann Arbor, MI: Center for the Improvement of Early Reading Achievement, University of Michigan.

Dickinson, D.K., & Smith, M.W. (1994). Long-term effects of preschool teachers' book readings on low-income children's vocabulary and story comprehension. *Reading Research Quarterly, 29*(2), 104–122.

Dickinson, D.K., & Tabors, P.O. (2002). Fostering language and literacy in classrooms and homes: Supporting language learning. *Young Children, 57*, 10–18.

Dodge, D.T., Colker, L.J., & Heroman, C. (2002). *The Creative Curriculum® for Preschool (4th ed.).* Washington, DC: Teaching Strategies, Inc.

Duke, N. (2004). The case for information text. *Educational Leadership, 61*(6), 40.

Dunn, L., Beach, S.A., & Kontos, S. (1994). Quality of the literacy environment in day care and children's development. *Journal of Research in Childhood Education, 9*, 24–34.

Early Childhood-Head Start Task Force. (2002). *Teaching our youngest: A guide for preschool teachers and child care and family providers.* Washington, DC: U.S. Department of Education.

Gelman, S.A., Wilcox, S.A., & Clark, E.V. (1989). Conceptual and lexical hierarchies in young children. *Cognitive Development, 4*, 309–326.

Genishi, C., & Dyson, A.H. (2009). *Children, language and literacy.* New York: Teachers College Press.

Gilhooly, K.J. (1984). Word age-of-acquisition and residence time in lexical memory as factors in word naming. *Current Psychological Research and Reviews, 3*, 24–31.

Girolametto, L., Weitzman, E., & Greenberg, J. (2006). Facilitating language skills. *Infants & Young Children, 19*(1), 36–49.

Golinkoff, R.M., Mervis, C.B., & Hirsh-Pasek, K. (1994). Early object labels: The case for a developmental lexical principles framework. *Journal of Child Language, 21*, 125–155.

Good, R.H., & Kaminski, R.A. (Eds.). (2002). *Dynamic Indicators of Basic Early Literacy Skills* (6th ed.).

Eugene, OR: Institute for the Development of Educational Achievement. Retrieved June 8, 2005, from http://dibels.uoregon.edu/

Goodson, B., Wolf, A., Bell, S., Turner, H., & Finney, P.B. (2010). *The effectiveness of a program to accelerate vocabulary development in kindergarten (VCAB).* (NCEE 2010-4014). Washington, DC: National Center for Education Evaluation and Regional Assistance, Institute for Education Sciences, U.S. Department of Education.

Hart, B., & Risley, T.R. (1995). *Meaningful differences in the everyday experience of young American children.* Baltimore: Paul H. Brookes Publishing Co.

Heroman, C., Burts, D.C., Berke, K., & Bickart, T. (2010). *The Creative Curriculum® for Preschool, Volume 5: Objectives for Development & Learning* (5th ed.) (pp. x-xii). Washington, DC: Teaching Strategies, Inc.

Heroman, C., Burts, D.C., Berke, K., & Bickart, T. (2010). *Teaching Strategies GOLD™ Objectives for Development & Learning: Birth Through Kindergarten* (pp. xxv–xxvii). Washington, DC: Teaching Strategies, Inc.

Hoff-Ginsberg, E. (1990). Maternal speech and the child's development of syntax: A further look. *Journal of Child Language, 17*, 85–99.

Hohman, M., Weikart, D. P., & Epstein, A. S. (2008). *Educating young children: Active learning practices for preschool and child care programs* (3rd ed.). Ypsilanti, MI: High Scope Press.

Howes, C., Hamilton, C.E., & Phillipsen, L.C. (1998). Stability and continuity of child-caregiver and child-peer relationships. *Child Development, 69*, 418–426.

Individuals with Disabilities Education Act of 1990, PL 101-476, 20 U.S.C. §§ 1400 *et seq.*

Juel, C. (1988). Learning to read and write: A longitudinal study of 54 children from first through fourth grades. *Journal of Educational Psychology, 80*, 437–447.

Justice, L.M., & Kaderavek, J. (2002). Using shared storybook reading to promote emergent literacy. *Teaching Exceptional Children, 34*(4), 8–13.

Kaminski, R.A., & Good, R.H. (1998). Assessing early literacy skills in a problem-solving model: Dynamic Indicators of Basic Early Literacy Skills. In M.R. Shinn (Ed.), *Advanced applications of curriculum-based measurement* (pp. 113–142). New York: Guilford Press.

Layzer, J., Goodson, B., & Moss, M. (1993). *Life in preschool: Volume one of an observational study of early childhood programs for disadvantaged four-year-olds.* Cambridge, MA: Abt Associates.

Lynch, J.S., Van den Broek, P., Kremer, K.E., Kendeou, P., White, M.J., & Lorch, E.P. (2008). The development of narrative comprehension and its relation to other early reading skills. *Reading Psychology, 29*, 327–365.

Mashburn, A.J., Hamre, B.K., Downer, J.T., & Pianta, R.C. (2006). Teacher and classroom characteristics associated with teachers' ratings of pre-kindergartners' relationships and behaviors. *Journal of Psychoeducational Assessment, 24*, 367–380.

Mashburn, A.J., Pianta, R.C., & Hamre, B.K. (2008). Measures of classroom quality in prekindergarten and children's development of academic, language and socials skills. *Child Development, 79*, 732–749.

McCartney, K. (1984). Effect of quality of day care environment on children's language development. *Developmental Psychology, 20,* 244–260.

Mervis, C.B. (1987). Child-basic object categories and early lexical development. In U. Neisser (Ed.), *Concepts and conceptual development: Ecological and intellectual factors in categorization* (pp. 201–233). Cambridge, England: Cambridge University Press.

Metsala, J. (1999). The development of phonemic awareness in reading-disabled children. *Applied Psycholinguistics, 20,* 149–158.

Miller, G., & Gildea, P. (1987). How children learn words. *Scientific American, 257*(3), 94–99.

Mol, S.F., Bus, A.G., & de Jong, M.T. (2009). Interactive book reading in early education: A tool to stimulate print knowledge as well as oral language. *Review of Educational Research, 79,* 979–1007.

Morrow, L.M. (2005). *Literacy development in the early years: Helping children read and write* (5th ed.). Boston: Allyn & Bacon.

Morrow, L.M., Kuhn, M.R., & Schwanenflugel, P.J. (2006). The family fluency program. *The Reading Teacher, 60,* 322–333.

Muter, V., Hulme, C., Snowling, M.J., & Stevenson, J. (2004). Phonemes, rimes, vocabulary, and grammatical skills as foundations of early reading development: Evidence from a longitudinal study. *Developmental Psychology, 40,* 665–681.

Nation, K., & Snowling, M.J. (2004). Beyond phonological skills: Broader language skills contribute to the development of reading. *Journal of Research in Reading, 27,* 342–356.

National Center for Education Statistics. (2010). *The condition of education 2000–2010.* Retrieved from http://nces.ed.gov/programs/coe/index.asp

National Center on Universal Design for Learning. (2010). *UDL guidelines—Version 1.* Retrieved from http://www.udlcenter.org/aboutudl/udlguidelines

National Early Literacy Panel. (2009). *Developing early literacy: Report of the National Early Literacy Panel.* Washington, DC: National Institute for Literacy.

National Governors Association. (2010). *State standards initiative: Common core.* Retrieved from http://www.corestandards.org/about-the-standards

National Institute of Child Health and Human Development Early Child Care Research Network. (2005). Pathways to reading: The role of oral language in the transition to reading. *Developmental Psychology, 41,* 428–444.

Neuman, S.B., & Celano, D. (2001). Access to print in low-income and middle-income communities: An ecological study of four neighborhoods. *Reading Research Quarterly, 36*(1), 8–26.

Paris, S.G. (2005). Reinterpreting the development of reading skills. *Reading Research Quarterly, 40*(2), 184–202.

Phillips, L.B., & Twardosz, S. (2003). Group size and storybook reading: Two-year-old children's verbal and nonverbal participation with books. *Early Education & Development, 14,* 453–478.

Price, L.H., van Kleeck, A., & Huberty, C.J. (2009). Talk during book sharing between parents and preschool children: A comparison between storybook and expository book conditions. *Reading Research Quarterly, 44*(2), 171–194.

Restrepo, M.A., & Dubasik, V. (2008). Language and literacy practices for English language learners in the preschool settings. In L.M. Justice & C. Vukelich (Eds.), *Achieving excellence in preschool literacy instruction* (pp. 242–260). New York: Guilford Press.

Roberts, J.E., Bailey, D.B., & Nychka, H.B. (1991). Teachers' use of strategies to facilitate the communication of preschool children with disabilities. *Journal of Early Intervention, 15,* 358–376.

Roskos, K.A., Tabors, P.O., & Lenhard, L.A. (2009). *Oral language and early literacy in preschool.* Newark, DE: International Reading Association.

Ruston, H.P., & Schwanenflugel, P.J. (2010). Effects of a conversation intervention on expressive vocabulary development of prekindergarten children. *Language, Speech, and Hearing Services in Schools, 41,* 303–310.

Scarborough, H. (1990). Very early language deficits in dyslexic children. *Child Development, 61,* 1728–1743.

Schwanenflugel, P.J. (1991). Why are abstract concepts hard to understand? In P.J. Schwanenflugel (Ed.), *The psychology of word meanings* (pp. 223–250). Mahwah, NJ: Lawrence Erlbaum Associates.

Schwanenflugel, P.J., Hamilton, C.E., Neuharth-Pritchett, S., Restrepo, M.A., Bradley, B.A., & Webb, M.-Y. (2010). *PAVEd for Success:* An evaluation of a comprehensive literacy program for 4-year-old children. *Journal of Literacy Research, 42*(3), 227–275.

Schwanenflugel, P.J., & Noyes, C.R. (1996). Context availability and the development of word reading skill. *Journal of Literacy Research, 28,* 35–54.

Schwanenflugel, P.J., Stahl, S.A., & McFalls, E.L. (1997). Partial word knowledge and vocabulary growth during reading comprehension. *Journal of Literacy Research, 29,* 531–553.

Senechal, M. (1997). The differential effect of storybook reading on preschoolers' acquisition of expressive and receptive vocabulary. *Journal of Child Language, 24,* 123–138.

Senechal, M., Thomas, E., & Monker, J.-A. (1995). Individual differences in 4-year-old children's acquisition of vocabulary during storybook reading. *Journal of Educational Psychology, 87,* 218–229.

SERVE Center. (2010). *The effectiveness of a program to accelerate vocabulary development in kindergarten (K-PAVE).* Retrieved from http://www.serve.org/KPAVEd.aspx

Snow, C., Burns, M., & Griffin, P. (1999). *Language and literacy environments in preschools.* Champaign, IL: ERIC Clearinghouse on Elementary and Early Childhood Education. (ERIC Documentation Service No. ED426818)

Stahl, K.A.D. (2007). Creating opportunities for comprehension instruction within fluency-oriented reading. In M. Kuhn & P.J. Schwanenflugel (Eds.), *Fluency in the classroom* (pp. 55–74). New York: Guilford Press.

Stahl, S.A. (1999). *Vocabulary development.* Cambridge, MA: Brookline Books.

Storch, S.A., & Whitehurst, G.J. (2002). Oral language and code-related precursors to reading: Evidence from a longitudinal structural model. *Developmental Psychology, 38,* 934–947.

Tabors, P.O. (2008). *One child, two languages: A guide for early childhood educators of children learning English as a second language* (2nd ed.). Baltimore: Paul H. Brookes Publishing Co.

Valdez-Menchaca, M.C., & Whitehurst, G.J. (1992). Accelerating language development through picture book reading: A systematic extension to Mexican day care. *Developmental Psychology, 28,* 1106–1114.

van Kleeck, A. (2003). Research on book sharing: Another critical look. In A. van Kleeck, S. Stahl, & E. Bauer (Eds.), *On reading books to children: Parents and teachers* (pp. 271–319). Mahwah, NJ: Lawrence Erlbaum Associates.

Verhoeven, L., & van Leeuwe, J. (2008). Prediction of the development of reading comprehension: A longitudinal study. *Applied Cognitive Psychology, 22,* 407–423.

Vukelich, C.V., & Christie, J. (2004). *Building a foundation for preschool literacy.* Newark, DE: International Reading Association.

Wasik, B.A., & Bond, M.A. (2001). Beyond the pages of a book: Interactive book reading and language development in preschool classrooms. *Journal of Educational Psychology, 93,* 243–250.

Wasik, B.A., Bond, M.A., & Hindman, A. (2006). The effects of a language and literacy intervention on Head Start children and teachers. *Journal of Educational Psychology, 98,* 63–74.

Wells, G. (1986). *The meaning makers: Children learning language and using language to learn.* Portsmouth, NH: Heinemann.

Wells, G., & Wells, J. (1984). Learning to talk and talking to learn. *Theory into Practice, 23*(3), 190–197.

Whitehurst, G.J., Arnold, D.H., Epstein, J.N., Angell, A.L., Smith, M., & Fischel, J.E. (1994). A picture book reading intervention in day care and home for children from low-income families. *Developmental Psychology, 30,* 679–689.

Whitehurst, G.J., Falco, F.L., Lonigan, C.J., Fischer, J.E., DeBaryshe, B.D., Valdez-Menchaca, M.C., et al. (1988). Accelerating language development through picture book reading. *Developmental Psychology, 24,* 552–559.

Whitehurst, G.J., & Lonigan, C.J. (1998). Child development and emergent literacy. *Child Development, 69,* 848–872.

Wilcox-Herzog, A.S., & Kontos, S. (1998). The nature of teacher talk in early childhood classrooms and its relationship to children's play with objects and peers. *Journal of Genetic Psychology, 159,* 30–44.

## CITED CHILDREN'S LITERATURE

Bang, M. (1999). *When Sophie gets angry—really, really angry….* New York: Blue Sky Press.

Bridwell, N. (2005). *Clifford the firehouse dog.* New York: Scholastic.

Cain, J. (2000). *The way I feel.* Seattle: Parenting Press.

Demarest, C.L. (2001). *Firefighters A to Z.* New York: Scholastic.

Herbert, M.P. (1992). *Rainbow fish.* New York: North-South Books.

McCloskey, R. (1948). *Blueberries for Sal.* New York: Penguin.

Rosinsky, N. (2003). *Magnets: Pulling together, pushing apart.* Minneapolis, MN: Picture Window Books.

Sherman, J. (2004). *Sunshine: A book about sunlight.* Minneapolis, MN: Picture Window Books.

APPENDIX

# A
- - -

# Alignment with Standards

*PAVEd for Success* aligns with the preschool program goals identified for the *Teaching Strategies GOLD™ Objectives for Development & Learning,* the Head Start Child Development and Early Learning Framework, and the *HighScope Preschool Curriculum* Content. The learning goals within these different programs are broad and are related to child social-emotional and physical development domains, among others. Here we address alignment only with the relevant areas of each program.

*PAVEd for Success* also meets most of the standards addressed in the Common Core State Standards for English Language Arts. These reflect content standards for kindergarten in three areas: 1) Reading: Literature and Informational Text, 2) Speaking and Listening, and 3) Reading: Foundational Skills. Reading: Foundational Skills is based on code-related skills and is not included here.

Individual PAVE vocabulary units meet national standards established for kindergarten science and social studies content. Included here is the alignment of individual vocabulary units with the National Science Education Standards and the National Council for the Social Studies Curriculum Strands.

## TEACHING STRATEGIES GOLD™ OBJECTIVES FOR DEVELOPMENT & LEARNING

*The Teaching Strategies GOLD™ Objectives for Development & Learning* (Heroman, Burts, Berke, & Bickart, 2010) includes 36 objectives organized into nine developmental areas. The alignment between *PAVEd for Success* and the areas of Language Development, Literacy, Science and Technology, and Social Studies is shown here. The dots indicate that the specific objective is addressed in PAVE.

| Language Development | Objectives addressed in *PAVEd for Success* |
|---|---|
| 8. Listens to and understands increasingly complex language | • |
| 9. Uses language to express thoughts and needs | • |
| 10. Uses appropriate conversational and other communication skills | • |

*(continued)*

*(continued)*

| Literacy | |
|---|:---:|
| 15. Demonstrates phonological awareness | |
| 16. Demonstrates knowledge of the alphabet | |
| 17. Demonstrates knowledge of print and its uses | • |
| 18. Comprehends and responds to books and other texts | • |
| 19. Demonstrates emergent writing skills | |
| **Science and Technology** | |
| 24. Uses scientific inquiry skills | • |
| 25. Demonstrates knowledge of the characteristics of living things | • |
| 26. Demonstrates knowledge of the physical properties of objects and materials | • |
| 27. Demonstrates knowledge of the Earth's environment | • |
| 28. Uses tools and other technology to perform tasks | |
| **Social Studies** | |
| 29. Demonstrates knowledge about self | |
| 30. Shows basic understanding of people and how they live | • |
| 31. Explores change related to familiar people or places | • |
| 32. Demonstrate simple geographic knowledge | • |

From *Teaching Strategies GOLD™ Objectives for Development & Learning: Birth Through Kindergarten* (pp. xxv–xxviii), and *The Creative Curriculum® for Preschool, Volume 5: Objectives for Development & Learning* (5th ed.), (pp. x–xii), by C. Heroman, D.C. Burts, Ed.D.; K. Berke, and T. Bickart, 2010, Washington, DC: Teaching Strategies, Inc. Copyright © 2010 by Teaching Strategies, Inc. Reprinted with permission.

# HEAD START CHILD DEVELOPMENT AND EARLY LEARNING FRAMEWORK

The Head Start Child Development and Early Learning Framework[a] is composed of 10 domains with an additional domain specifically addressing the needs of dual language learners. The alignment between *PAVEd for Success* and Language Development, Literacy Knowledge and Skills, Science Knowledge and Skills, and English Language Development is shown here.

| Domain | Domain element | Elements addressed in *PAVEd for Success* |
|---|---|:---:|
| Language Development | **Receptive Language**<br><br>The ability to comprehend or understand language. | • |
| | **Expressive Language**<br><br>The ability to use language. | • |
| Literacy Knowledge & Skills | **Book Appreciation and Knowledge**<br><br>The interest in books and their characteristics, and the ability to understand and get meaning from stories and information books and other texts. | • |

*(continued)*

*(continued)*

|  | Phonological Awareness<br><br>An awareness that language can be broken into words, syllables, and smaller pieces of sound. |  |
|---|---|---|
|  | Alphabet Knowledge<br><br>The names and sounds associated with letters. |  |
|  | Print Concepts and Conventions<br><br>The concepts about print and early decoding (identifying letter-sound relationships). |  |
|  | Early Writing<br><br>The familiarity with writing implements, conventions, and emerging skills to communicate through written representation, symbols, and letters. |  |
| Science Knowledge & Skills[b] | Scientific Skills and Method<br><br>The skills to observe and collect information and use it to ask questions, predict, explain, and draw conclusions. | • |
|  | Conceptual Knowledge of the Natural and Physical World<br><br>The acquisition of concepts and facts related to the natural and physical world and the understanding of naturally occurring relationships. | • |
| Social Studies Knowledge & Skills[b] | Self, Family and Community<br><br>The understanding of one's relationship to the family and community, roles in the family and community, and respect for diversity. | • |
|  | People and the Environment<br><br>The understanding of the relationship between people and the environment in which they live. | • |
|  | History and Events<br><br>The understanding that events happened in the past and how these events relate to one's self, family and community. | • |
| English Language Development<br>(This domain applies only to dual language learners.) | Receptive English Language Skills<br><br>The ability to comprehend or understand the English Language. | • |
|  | Expressive English Language Skills<br><br>The ability to speak or use English. | • |
|  | Engagement in English Literacy Activities<br><br>Understanding and responding to books, storytelling, and songs represented in English. | • |

[a]From *The Head Start Child Development and Early Learning Framework: Promoting Positive Outcomes in Early Childhood Programs Serving Children 3–5 Years Old*. HHS/ACF/OHS. 2010. English.

[b]The *PAVEd for Success* program as a whole does not address all of the science or social studies skills; nonetheless, many skills are addressed within the individual unit.

## *HIGHSCOPE PRESCHOOL CURRICULUM* CONTENT— KEY DEVELOPMENTAL INDICATORS

The *HighScope Preschool Curriculum* Content—Key Developmental Indicators (http://www. highscope.org/Content.asp?ContentId=566) are organized around eight areas: 1) Approaches to Learning; 2) Social and Emotional Development; 3) Physical Development and Health; 4) Language, Literacy, and Communication; 5) Mathematics; 6) Creative Arts; 7) Science and Technology; and 8) Social Studies. The alignment between *PAVEd for Success* and Language, Literacy, and Communication; Science and Technology; and Social Studies is shown here.

| Domain | Domains addressed in *PAVEd for Success* |
|---|:---:|
| **D. Language, Literacy, and Communication** | |
| 21. Comprehension: Children understand language. | • |
| 22. Speaking: Children express themselves using language. | • |
| 23. Vocabulary: Children understand and use a variety of words and phrases. | • |
| 24. Phonological awareness: Children identify distinct sounds in spoken language. | |
| 25. Alphabetic knowledge: Children identify letter names and their sounds. | |
| 26. Reading: Children read for pleasure and information. | • |
| 27. Concepts about print: Children demonstrate knowledge about environmental print. | |
| 28. Book knowledge: Children demonstrate knowledge about books. | • |
| 29. Writing: Children write for many different purposes. | |
| 30. [English language learning]/Dual language acquisition: (if applicable) Children use English and their home language(s). | • |
| **G. Science and Technology**[a] | |
| 45. Observing: Children observe the materials and processes in their environment. | • |
| 46. Classifying: Children classify materials, actions, people, and events. | • |
| 47. Experimenting: Children experiment to test their new ideas. | • |
| 48. Predicting: Children predict what they expect will happen. | • |
| 49. Drawing conclusions: Children draw conclusions based on their experiences and observations. | • |
| 50. Communicating ideas: Children communicate their ideas about the characteristics of things and how they work. | • |
| 51. Natural and physical world: Children gather knowledge about the natural and physical world. | • |
| 52. Tools and technology: Children explore and use tools and technology. | |
| **H. Social Studies**[b] | |
| 53. Diversity: Children understand that people have diverse characteristics, interests, and abilities. | • |
| 54. Community roles: Children recognize that people have different roles and functions in the community. | • |
| 55. Decision making: Children participate in making classroom decisions. | |
| 56. Geography: Children recognize and interpret features and locations in their environment. | • |
| 57. History: Children understand past, present, and future. | • |
| 58. Ecology: Children understand the importance of taking care of their environment. | • |

[a]Content is covered in specific PAVE units. See the National Science Education Standards for alignment between vocabulary units and content areas.

[b]Content is covered in specific PAVE units. See the National Council for the Social Studies Strands for alignment between vocabulary units and content areas.

# COMMON CORE STATE STANDARDS FOR ENGLISH LANGUAGE ARTS

*PAVEd for Success* meets many of the standards addressed in the Common Core State Standards for English Language (http://www.corestandards.org/the-standards/english-language-arts-standards). These reflect content standards for kindergarten in three areas: 1) Reading: Literature and Informational Text, 2) Speaking and Listening, and 3) Reading: Foundational Skills. Reading: Foundational Skills is based on code-related skills and is not included here.

| Domain | Domains addressed in *PAVEd for Success* |
|---|:---:|
| **Reading: Literature** | |
| **Key Ideas and Details** | |
| RL.K.1. With prompting and support, ask and answer questions about key details in a text. | • |
| RL.K.2. With prompting and support, retell familiar stories, including key details. | |
| RL.K.3. With prompting and support, identify characters, settings, and major events in a story. | • |
| **Craft and Structure** | |
| RL.K.4. Ask and answer questions about unknown words in a text. | • |
| RL.K.5. Recognize common types of texts (e.g., storybooks, poems). | • |
| RL.K.6. With prompting and support, name the author and illustrator and define the role of each in telling the story. | |
| **Integration of Knowledge and Ideas** | |
| RL.K.7. With prompting and support, describe the relationship between illustrations and the story in which they appear (e.g., what moment in a story an illustration depicts). | • |
| RL.K.8. (Not applicable to literature) | |
| RL.K.9. With prompting and support, compare and contrast the adventures and experiences of characters in familiar stories. | • |
| **Range of Reading and Level of Text Complexity** | |
| RL.K.10. Actively engage in group reading activities with purpose and understanding. | • |
| **Reading: Informational Text** | |
| **Key Ideas and Details** | |
| RI.K.1. With prompting and support, ask and answer questions about key details in a text. | • |
| RI.K.2. With prompting and support, identify the main topic and retell key details of a text. | • |
| RI.K.3. With prompting and support, describe the connection between two individuals, events, ideas, or pieces of information in a text. | • |
| **Craft and Structure** | |
| RI.K.4. With prompting and support, ask and answer questions about unknown words in a text. | • |
| RI.K.5. Identify the front cover, back cover, and title page of a book. | |
| RI.K.6. Name the author and illustrator of a text and define the role of each in presenting the ideas or information in a text. | |
| **Integration of Knowledge and Ideas** | |
| RI.K.7. With prompting and support, describe the relationship between illustrations and the text in which they appear (e.g., what person, place, thing, or idea in the text an illustration depicts) | • |
| RI.K.8. With prompting and support, identify the reasons an author gives to support points in a text. | |
| RI.K.9. With prompting and support, identify basic similarities and differences between two texts on the same topic (e.g., in illustrations, descriptions, or procedures). | • |

*(continued)*

(continued)

| Range of Reading and Level of Text Complexity | |
|---|---|
| RI.K.10. Actively engage in group reading activities with purpose and understanding. | • |
| **Speaking and Listening** | |
| **Comprehension and Collaboration** | |
| SL.K.1. Participate in collaborative conversations with diverse partners about *kindergarten topics and texts* with peers and adults in small and larger groups.<br>• Follow agreed-upon rules for discussions (e.g., listening to others and taking turns speaking about the topics and texts under discussion).<br>• Continue a conversation through multiple exchanges. | • |
| SL.K.2. Confirm understanding of a text read aloud or information presented orally or through other media by asking and answering questions about key details and requesting clarification if something is not understood. | • |
| SL.K.3. Ask and answer questions in order to seek help, get information, or clarify that something is not understood. | • |
| **Presentation of Knowledge and Ideas** | |
| SL.K.4. Describe familiar people, places, things, and events and, with prompting and support, provide additional detail. | • |
| SL.K.5. Add drawings or other visual displays to descriptions as desired to provide additional detail. | • |
| SL.K.6. Speak audibly and express thoughts, feelings, and ideas clearly. | • |
| **Language** | |
| **Conventions of Standard English** | |
| L.K.1. Demonstrate command of the conventions of standard English grammar and usage when writing or speaking<br>• Print many upper- and lowercase letters.<br>• Use frequently occurring nouns and verbs.<br>• Form regular plural nouns orally by adding /s/ or /es/ (e.g., *dog, dogs; wish, wishes*).<br>• Understand and use question words (interrogatives) (e.g., *who, what, where, when, why, how*).<br>• Use the most frequently occurring prepositions (e.g., *to, from, in, out, on, off, for, of, by, with*).<br>• Produce and expand complete sentences in shared language activities. | • |
| L.K.2. Demonstrate command of the conventions of standard English capitalization, punctuation, and spelling when writing<br>• Capitalize the first word in a sentence and the pronoun *I*.<br>• Recognize and name end punctuation.<br>• Write a letter or letters for most consonant and short-vowel sounds (phonemes).<br>• Spell simple words phonetically, drawing on knowledge of sound-letter relationships. | |
| **Knowledge of Language** | |
| L.K.3. (Begins in Grade 2) | |
| **Vocabulary Acquisition and Use** | |
| L.K.4. Determine or clarify the meaning of unknown words and multiple-meaning words and phrases based on kindergarten reading and content<br>• Identify new meanings for familiar words and apply them accurately (e.g., knowing *duck* is a bird and learning the verb to *duck*).<br>• Use the most frequently occurring inflections and affixes (e.g., *-ed, -s, re-, un-, pre-, -ful, -less*) as a clue to the meaning of an unknown word. | • |
| L.K.5. With guidance and support from adults, explore word relationships and nuances in word meanings<br>• Sort common objects into categories (e.g., shapes, foods) to gain a sense of the concepts the categories represent.<br>• Demonstrate understanding of frequently occurring verbs and adjectives by relating them to their opposites (antonyms).<br>• Identify real-life connections between words and their use (e.g., note places at school that are colorful).<br>• Distinguish shades of meaning among verbs describing the same general action (e.g., *walk, march, strut, prance*) by acting out the meanings. | • |
| L.K.6. Use words and phrases acquired through conversations, reading and being read to, and responding to texts. | • |

# NATIONAL SCIENCE EDUCATION STANDARDS

Alignment between individual *PAVEd for Success* vocabulary units and the National Science Education Standards for kindergarten through Grade 4 (http://www.nap.edu/openbook.php?record_id=4962&page=R1) is shown here. Alignment between the PAVE science units and the different National Science Education Standards are indicated with a • . Some of the social studies units also include topics and activities relevant to the science content standards; these are noted with a ✓.

| PAVE unit | Science as Inquiry | Physical Science | Life Science | Earth and Space Science | Science and Technology | Science in Personal and Social Perspectives | History and Nature of Science |
|---|---|---|---|---|---|---|---|
| **Science units** | | | | | | | |
| Animal Babies | | | • | | | | |
| Bug Helpers | | | • | | | | |
| Dental Health | | | | | | • | |
| Feelings | | | | | | • | |
| Gardening | • | | • | | | | |
| Living in the Earth: Worms and Pillbugs | | | • | | | | |
| Magnets | • | • | | | | | |
| Outer Space | | | | • | | | |
| Recycling and the Environment | | | | • | | • | |
| Solids, Liquids, and Gases | | • | | | | • | |
| Trains and Bridges | | | | | • | | |
| Transportation | | | | | • | | |
| **Integrated science and social studies units** | | | | | | | |
| Food Preparation | | ✓ | | | | | |
| Landforms | | | | ✓ | | ✓ | |
| Primary Land Uses | | | | ✓ | | ✓ | |
| Seasons | | | ✓ | ✓ | | | |
| Weather | | | | ✓ | | | |
| Winter | | | | ✓ | | | |

# NATIONAL COUNCIL FOR THE SOCIAL STUDIES CURRICULUM STRANDS

Alignment between individual *PAVEd for Success* vocabulary social studies units and the National Council for the Social Studies Curriculum Strands (http://www.socialstudies.org/standards/strands) are indicated with a •. Some of the PAVE science units also include topics and activities relevant to the Social Studies Curriculum Strands; these are noted with ✓.

| PAVE unit | Culture | Time, Continuity, & Change | People, Places, & Environments | Individual Development & Identity | Individuals, Groups, & Institutions | Power, Authority, & Governance | Production, Distribution, & Consumption | Science, Technology, & Society | Global Connections | Civic Ideals & Practices |
|---|---|---|---|---|---|---|---|---|---|---|
| **Social studies units** | | | | | | | | | | |
| Hooray for School! | | | • | | • | | | | | |
| Careers and Community Helpers | | | | • | | | • | | | |
| Fire Safety | | | | | | | • | | | |
| Food Preparation | • | | • | | | | | | | |
| Landforms | | | • | | | | | | | |
| Maps and Globes | | | • | | | | | | | |
| Medieval Times | | • | | | | | | | | |
| Music | • | • | | | | | | | | |
| Primary Land Uses | | | • | | • | | • | | | |
| Seasons | | • | • | • | | | | | | |
| Weather | | | • | | | | | | | |
| Winter | • | | • | | | | | | | |
| **Integrated social studies and science units** | | | | | | | | | | |
| Dental Health | | | | | | | ✓ | | | |
| Outer Space | | | ✓ | | | | | | | |
| Recycling and the Environment | | | ✓ | | | | | ✓ | | |
| Trains and Bridges | | ✓ | | | | | | ✓ | | |
| Transportation | ✓ | | ✓ | | | | | | | |

# B

# Resources and Tools

# Student Tracking Tool

Week of: _____

Instructions: Place a ✓ in the appropriate box as the child engages in each of the activities.

| Child name | Building Bridges sessions | | | CAR Quest small-group reading | | | New VEhicles Extension activity | |
|---|---|---|---|---|---|---|---|---|
| | 1 | 2 | 3 | 1 | 2 | 3 | 1 | 2 |
| 1. | | | | | | | | |
| 2. | | | | | | | | |
| 3. | | | | | | | | |
| 4. | | | | | | | | |
| 5. | | | | | | | | |
| 6. | | | | | | | | |
| 7. | | | | | | | | |
| 8. | | | | | | | | |
| 9. | | | | | | | | |
| 10. | | | | | | | | |
| 11. | | | | | | | | |
| 12. | | | | | | | | |
| 13. | | | | | | | | |
| 14. | | | | | | | | |
| 15. | | | | | | | | |
| 16. | | | | | | | | |
| 17. | | | | | | | | |
| 18. | | | | | | | | |
| 19. | | | | | | | | |
| 20. | | | | | | | | |
| 21. | | | | | | | | |
| 22. | | | | | | | | |
| 23. | | | | | | | | |
| 24. | | | | | | | | |
| 25. | | | | | | | | |
| 26. | | | | | | | | |
| 27. | | | | | | | | |
| 28. | | | | | | | | |
| 29. | | | | | | | | |
| 30. | | | | | | | | |

# Teacher Checklist

Week: _____

Date: _____

Instructions: Review each of the *PAVEd for Success* components. If you were unable to fully implement one of the components this week, consider what strategies will help you meet the program goals.

| PAVE component | Strategies to meet program goals |
|---|---|
| 1. *Building Bridges:* Child-Centered Conversation<br>❑ Children were engaged in conversations centered on their interests and topics.<br>❑ Children were allowed significant opportunity to talk. | |
| 2. *Building Bridges:* Sufficient Conversation Duration<br>❑ Children had a small-group[a] conversation with me or another adult[b] that lasted at least 5 minutes.<br>❑ Children were engaged in three such conversations this week. | |
| 3. *Building Bridges:* Linguistically Complex Talk<br>❑ Children had their simple speech expanded on with language expansions or questions that encouraged interpreting, hypothesizing, clarifying, open-ended questions (e.g., how, why, what else).<br>❑ Children heard their simple words expanded on by the adult through the use of complex vocabulary words (dime words) as a natural part of the Building Bridges conversations. | |
| 4. *CAR Quest:* Competence Questions<br>❑ In book read-alouds, children were asked *two* questions for which they could demonstrate their competence (things they were likely to know, such as "Who said...?" or "Where is...?"). | |
| 5. *CAR Quest:* Abstract Questions<br>❑ In read-alouds, children were asked *two* questions for which they could demonstrate their ability to think abstractly (e.g., "Why do you think...?" or "What will happen...?"). | |
| 6. *CAR Quest:* Relate Questions<br>❑ In read-alouds, children were asked *two* questions for which they could relate the book to their lives. | |

[a]*Small group* in all instances means a group size of seven or fewer. English language learners or children with special needs might participate in smaller groups.
[b]This other adult can be a trained assistant teacher, volunteer, literacy coach, or inclusion teacher.

*(continued)*

## Teacher Checklist (continued)

| PAVE component | Strategies to meet program goals |
|---|---|
| 7. *CAR Quest* Scheduling<br>❑ Children were engaged in three small-group read-alouds this week.<br>❑ Children participated in five large-group read-aloud sessions. | |
| 8. *New VEhicles*: Quick Definitions<br>❑ Children heard quick definitions when vocabulary words were introduced. | |
| 9. *New VEhicles*: Novel Name–Nameless Category (N3C) Introduction or Review of Vocabulary<br>❑ Vocabulary words were introduced using the N3C strategy.<br>❑ Vocabulary words were reviewed by asking children to name or pick out the appropriate vocabulary picture card on subsequent days. | |
| 10. *New VEhicles*: Communication<br>❑ The week's vocabulary words were posted in the classroom.<br>❑ Parents were sent the vocabulary word list and unit topic. | |
| 11. *New VEhicles*: Extension Activity<br>❑ Children participated in *two* extension activities to encourage the use of the vocabulary words. | |
| 12. *New VEhicles*: Sufficient Small-Group Extension Activity Quantity<br>❑ Children participated in at least *two* small-group extension activities this week. | |

# Coach/Supervisor
# Observation Checklist Instructions

Effective professional development should be supportive, intensive, and continuous, with individualized feedback and positive mentoring. This checklist is designed for a 90-minute classroom observation. The teacher should provide a class schedule indicating when *PAVEd for Success* is typically carried out in the classroom. If the teacher uses an assistant to carry out significant parts of the program, the assistant should also be observed.

1. *Building Bridges:* Child-Centered Conversation

    The purpose of this component is to provide conversations that build oral language skills and good teacher–student relationships through talk.

    a. Children's interests or topics should be focused on in these conversations. The teacher should not reteach other topics within the curriculum in these conversations.

    b. Children should have a significant opportunity to talk. The teacher should encourage children to elaborate.

2. *Building Bridges:* Sufficient Conversation Duration

    The goal of this component is to ensure that a sufficient amount of teacher–child conversation occurs to encourage the development of language skills.

    a. Small groups (seven children or fewer) should be at least *5 minutes* in duration.

    b. Groups can follow small-group activities, meals, or naps or occur before or after school.

    c. Ideally two sessions per observation should be observed. If only one is observed, then another occurring that day can be self-reported.

    d. There should be a schedule showing each child participating in at least three Building Bridges conversations per week.

3. *Building Bridges:* Linguistically Complex Talk

    The purpose of this component is to encourage teacher speech related to the development of oral language skills and vocabulary. It should characterize teacher speech.

    a. Complex talk
       i. Questions that query thoughts and feelings ("What was he feeling?"), require clarifying and hypothesizing ("What do you mean?" "What happened?"), and elicit talk ("How?" "Why?" "What else?").
       ii. Language expansions that add missing grammatical elements or elaborate on child speech. They should be noncorrective in tone so that the child is encouraged to speak (e.g., Child: "My daddy, he went Wal-Mart." → Teacher: "Your father went to Wal-Mart? Did he go to the one near the mall?").

    b. Emphasis on vocabulary
       i. Rare vocabulary introduced by the teacher in conversation (e.g., Child: "There a big car." → Teacher: "Oh, yes, that's an enormous car. Is that a sports utility vehicle?").

*(continued)*

# Coach/Supervisor Observation Checklist Instructions (continued)

4. *CAR Quest:* **Competence Questions**

   The purpose of these questions is to provide children with success in addressing some teacher questions and to encourage their participation during storybook reading.

   a. Classify a question as Competence if children would be expected to know the information being queried or if the information is directly in the book. A vocabulary word might be embedded, however.

   b. The teacher can be observed asking two questions of this type, or sticky notes containing the questions inserted in books can be used as evidence.

5. *CAR Quest:* **Abstract Questions**

   The purpose of these questions is to encourage cognitively and linguistically complex talk, which has been shown to improve vocabulary and comprehension.

   a. Classify a question as *abstract* if it asks students to summarize, define, explain, judge, compare, contrast, predict, take another point of view, or solve problems. "How" and "why" questions and questions about character thoughts are always abstract (e.g., "Why do you think [person] did [action]?" "What is [character] thinking?" "What does [word] mean?" "What will happen next?" "How are [two objects] different?" "What was the story about?").

   b. The teacher can be observed asking two questions of this type, or sticky notes with the questions inserted in books can be used as evidence.

6. *CAR Quest:* **Relate Questions**

   The purpose of these questions is to encourage children to relate the contents of books to their own lives and prior knowledge to promote comprehension.

   a. Classify a question as *relate* if it requires children to relate the contents of books to their own lives (e.g., "Have you ever had a really horrible day?" "What do you do when you have a bad dream?" "What would you do if you could [action] like Hager?" "Who has on a blue shirt like Oliver's?").

   b. The teacher can be observed asking two questions of this type, or sticky notes with the questions inserted in books can be used as evidence.

7. *CAR Quest:* **Sufficient Small-Group Book-Reading Quantity**

   The purpose of this component is to ensure that children have ample opportunity to learn vocabulary words from the books being read.

   a. Two small-group (group size of seven or fewer) book readings should occur.

   b. Ideally two sessions should be observed. If only one session is observed, then another self-reported one occurring that day can be used as evidence.

   c. There should be a schedule showing each child participating in small-group book-reading sessions per week.

8. *New VEhicles:* **Quick Definitions**

   The purpose of this component is to get children familiar with thinking about definitions for words, a skill under development at this age.

   a The teacher should supply kid-friendly definitions of vocabulary words or any words.

   b. This can be self-reported.

*(continued)*

# Coach/Supervisor Observation Checklist Instructions (continued)

9. *New VEhicles:* N3C Introduction or Review of Vocabulary

    The purpose of this component is to provide children with a chance to exercise a strategy for learning new words already in their word-learning repertoire and to review previously introduced words.

    a. The teacher should present a vocabulary word picture card in the context of several known (nontarget) picture cards. The teacher should query each by saying, "Show me (vocabulary word)" or something similar.

    Or

    The teacher can review previously presented vocabulary words using picture cards and props by saying, "Which one is (vocabulary word)?" or something similar.

    b. If not observed, this can be self-reported.

10. *New VEhicles:* Presence of Vocabulary Targets

    The purpose of this component is to communicate to children that there is a list of words that they should be learning.

    a. The teacher should post vocabulary lists or picture cards or props of targets as a group somewhere in the room.

    b. The teacher should send home a parent communication indicating the vocabulary for the week.

11. *New VEhicles:* Extension Activity

    The purpose of this practice is to allow children to have the opportunity to practice the vocabulary words in some activity.

    a. Children should be sent to small-group (seven members or fewer) activities in which they are encouraged to process vocabulary words further.

12. *New VEhicles:* Sufficient Small-Group Extension Activity Quantity

    The purpose of this practice is to ensure that children have enough practice using the vocabulary words in an activity.

    a. Ideally, two groups should be observed, but if only one is observed, a second occurring that day can be self-reported.

    b. There should be a schedule showing each child participating in two small-group extension activities per week.

# Observation Checklist for Coach/Supervisor

**Teacher:** _____

**Date:** _____

Instructions: Review each of the program components. Circle "yes" or "no" in the left-hand column indicating whether the intervention was used, and use the space for follow-up notes if needed.

| Intervention component | Remediation required?<br>(Circle yes or no)<br>Notes for follow-up | |
| --- | --- | --- |
| 1. *Building Bridges:* Child-Centered Conversation<br>❐ Teacher[a] engaged children in conversations centered on children's interests and topics.<br>❐ Teacher allowed children a significant opportunity to talk.<br>*Note: Both components must be observed.* | Yes | No |
| 2. *Building Bridges:* Sufficient Conversation Duration<br>❐ Teacher engaged in at least *two* small-group[b] conversations. (Fill in number of minutes for each conversation observed.)<br>❐ Each conversation lasted 5 minutes.<br>❐ Evidence that three sessions per child are scheduled for the week. | Yes | No |
| 3. *Building Bridges:* Linguistically Complex Talk<br>❐ Complex talk: Teacher's conversations with children included questions that encouraged interpreting, hypothesizing, clarifying, open-ended questions (how, why, what else); and/or teacher carried out language expansions.<br>❐ Vocabulary emphasis—Teacher introduced rare vocabulary words in conversation.<br>*Note: Both aspects must be observed, but they can occur outside Building Bridges time.* | Yes | No |
| 4. *CAR Quest:* Competence Questions<br>❐ When reading a book to children, teacher asked *two* questions for which children could demonstrate competence (e.g., "Who said…?" "Where is…?").<br>*Note: Must be observed during book-reading times.* | Yes | No |
| 5. *CAR Quest:* Abstract Questions<br>❐ When reading a book to children, teacher asked *two* questions for which children could demonstrate their ability to think abstractly (e.g., "Why do you think…?" "What will happen…?").<br>*Note: Must be observed during book-reading times.* | Yes | No |

*(continued)*

*PAVEd for Success: Building Vocabulary and Language Development in Young Learners,* by Claire E. Hamilton & Paula J. Schwanenflugel.

# Observation Checklist for Coach/Supervisor (continued)

| Intervention component | Remediation required? (Circle yes or no) Notes for follow-up | |
|---|---|---|
| 6. *CAR Quest*: Relate Questions <br> ❑ When reading a book aloud, teacher asked *two* questions for which children could relate the book to their lives. <br> *Note: Must be observed during book-reading times.* | Yes | No |
| 7. *CAR Quest Scheduling* <br> ❑ Teacher carried out *two* small-group interactive readings of books. <br> ❑ Teacher has scheduled *three* small-group book-reading sessions for each child for the week. <br> *Note: If only one small-group reading is observed, the second for that day can be self-reported.* | Yes | No |
| 8. *New VEhicles*: Quick Definitions <br> ❑ Teacher supplied the definitions of vocabulary words or other words used. <br> *Note: If not observed, can be self-reported in the lesson plan.* | Yes | No |
| 9. *New VEhicles*: N3C Introduction or Review of Vocabulary <br> ❑ Teacher engaged children in a Novel Name–Nameless category (N3C) activity. <br> ❑ Teacher presented picture cards and asked for appropriate labels. <br> *Note: If not observed, can be self-reported in the lesson plan.* | Yes | No |
| 10. *New VEhicles*: Communication <br> ❑ Teacher posted a list of new vocabulary words. <br> *Note: Must be observed.* <br> ❑ Teacher sent home a list of new vocabulary words and the unit topic. <br> *Note: Can be self-reported.* | Yes | No |
| 11. *New VEhicles*: Extension Activity <br> ❑ Children engaged in *two* centers that encouraged the use of vocabulary words in activity. | Yes | No |
| 12. *New VEhicles*: Sufficient Small-Group Extension Activity Quantity <br> ❑ At least *two* small groups were observed in centers in which children could practice vocabulary. <br> ❑ Teacher has a schedule indicating that each child will participate in *two* extension activities per week. <br> *Note: If only one activity is observed, the second occurring that day can be self-reported in the lesson plan.* | Yes | No |

[a]*Teacher* in all instances means either the lead or assistant teacher.
[b]*Small group* in all instances means a group size of seven or fewer.

# Assessments of Children's Oral Language Skills

## LANGUAGE SAMPLE MEASUREMENT

If teachers want to assess how well a particular child's oral language is progressing, they could record that child's talk on a regular basis and determine whether there has been growth over the school year. We find that using a wordless storybook is an excellent way to get a sense of the progression of children's oral language. Indeed, there are now standardized procedures and norms available for doing this for education purposes. The Edmonton Narrative Norms Instrument (ENNI; Schneider, Dubé, & Hayward, 2004) has pictures and procedures for evaluating a sample of a child's language to determine progress. Teachers track changes in the average number of words per sentence and number of different words children use in their speech every few months. These measures have some validity in measuring children's progress up to age 5 or so, so they are more appropriate for use with prekindergarten than kindergarten children. If a child has known speech-language problems, the ENNI has validity for use a bit later than age 5. Teachers can also determine whether the stories children tell from these wordless picture prompts have all of the components of a complete story (e.g., a setting, characters, plot, resolution). This has some validity in describing oral language differences among children and showing growth from age 4 until ages 7–8 (Schneider, Hayward, & Dubé, 2006). The ENNI is available for educational use by teachers and speech-language professionals at http://www.languageanalysislab.com/salt/downloads/ENNIRDBDoc.pdf.

## THE TEACHER RATING OF ORAL LANGUAGE AND LITERACY

The Teacher Rating of Oral Language and Literacy (TROLL; Dickinson, McCabe, & Sprague, 2001) is designed for teachers to track children's oral language and literacy skills. Unlike standardized tests, it takes into account the fact that teachers often have a breadth of experience with particular children that may allow them to make an *accurate assessment* of children's knowledge, language, and early literacy skills. Designed to be a general literacy measure, the TROLL has three subscales: 1) Language Use, 2) Reading, and 3) Writing. The language use subscale in particular emphasizes many of the same points that the *PAVEd for Success* program does. Studies have shown the TROLL to be a reliable and reasonably valid measure of children's skills as determined by a comparison of teacher ratings and standardized tests. This instrument is available for educational use by teachers at http://www.ciera.org/library/reports/inquiry-3/3-016/3-016.pdf.

## REFERENCES

Dickinson, D. McCabe, A., & Sprague, K. (2001) *Teacher Rating of Oral Language and Literacy (TROLL)*. Ann Arbor, MI: Center for the Improvement of Early Reading Achievement (CIERA). http://www.ciera.org/library/reports/inquiry-3/3-016/3-016.pdf

Schneider, P., Dubé, R.V., & Hayward, D. (2004). The Edmonton Narrative Norms Instrument. Available at http://www.rehabmed.ualberta.ca/spa/enni/

Schneider, P., Hayward, D., & Dubé, R.V. (2006). Storytelling from pictures using the Edmonton Narrative Norms Instrument. *Journal of Speech-Language Pathology and Audiology, 30*, 224–238.